Pathway to Spirit

Pathway to Spirit

*A Journey to Clairvoyance
and
Spiritual Enlightenment*

Ann Caulfield

Zambezi Publishing

First published in the UK 2004
by Zambezi Publishing
P.O. Box 221 Plymouth,
Devon PL2 2YJ (UK)
Fax: +44 (0)1752 350 453
email: info@zampub.com
www.zampub.com

British Library Cataloguing in Publication Data:
A catalogue record for this book
is available from the British Library

ISBN 1-903065-35-6

Cover design: © 2004 Jan Budkowski
Photo: © 2004 Ann Caulfield
135798642

Printed in the UK by Lightning Source

Dedication

This book is dedicated to my daughter, Nicky, who
continues to encourage me from spirit.

Acknowledgments

It was my guide, Mothhawk, who first asked me to write this
book. Shortly after I had begun to put pen to paper, my
youngest daughter, Nicky, became seriously ill and
subsequently died. I lost heart in life itself for a while and the
book was put aside. When I was at my lowest point, she
made contact with me, proving beyond all doubt that she
lives on and is well and happy. Over the following months,
she inspired me to try again. Without her, my father, guides,
teachers and friends in spirit I would never have started. It is
to them that I give my loving thanks for leading me once
more through my psychic journey to spiritual enlightenment.

Despite their encouragement, I had to learn how to put
it all into words, so they guided me to a writing class.
Overawed by the quality of writing of the students, I almost
gave up after the first evening – but spirit thought otherwise.
They sent Della and Sandi to me, and both persuaded me to
stay. My tutor, Ian Burton, reassured me from the beginning
that I had a fascinating story to tell, and I will be forever
grateful to him and my fellow students for the positive
criticism and guidance that they gave me.

Special thanks also to David Wass, Marley, Eileen,
Barbara, Nancy, David Hough, Quinton and Josette for their
unwavering support in and out of class.

And how can I forget my extra-curricular manuscript evenings? Thanks to Della, Sandi, David and Adam, the food, wine and jokes helped the words to flow and kept us laughing.

For the unwavering support of other friends who pulled me back up whenever I felt low, they have my heartfelt gratitude. They could so easily have walked away. Paul Worple and Alison Hensridge-New, despite their personal problems, were always there for me. Thanks also to Daphne Helliwell, my close friend and sounding board, who had the painstaking but much appreciated job of checking every word of my manuscript. Dorothy Chapman, my fell medium, who took time out to revive memories of our early days of working together.

My special love and thanks to my eldest daughter, Karen, a published author herself, who told me never to give up. And of course, my husband, Peter, who proved to be a dab hand at cooking and who kept me fortified with a spirit of a different kind.

And finally, to Jan and Sasha of Zambezi Publishing, who believed enough in me to want to publish my story... a big, big thank you.

Foreword

"Art is the flower – life is the green leaf. Let every artist strive to make his flower a beautiful living thing – something that will convince the world that there may be – there are – things more precious – more beautiful – more lasting than life."
(From "Seemliness" 1902)
Charles Rennie Mackintosh

Ann Caulfield did not seek the psychic path – spirit directed her to it. Upon it lay the gift of mediumistic perception. However, with this gift came a heavy responsibility - indeed some may see it as a burden. In all the years that I have known her, she has carried it through, never complaining, even when it has drained her energies to the point of affecting her physical well-being.

Accepting this awesome gift, she retains the humility of a compassionate human being. When called upon to work outside her terrestrial sphere, she perceives herself as merely an interpreter and messenger. Does she always get it right? This is her greatest concern, and remains with her despite evidence of her numerous accurate readings. Later in this book, you will see that both Ann and her husband, Peter, held spiritual healing sessions some time ago. She continues to engage daily with such healing in absentia, embracing all those on her list.

Certain readers may be inclined to dismiss this life story as a fairy-tale. This is not so. It is very real, and even now, Ann continues along this demanding path. Her story, simply told, is interesting, informative and warmly human. However, it is more than that, because hers is two books in one. Part Two is a teaching book, setting out the steps in an orderly manner and pointing out the problems that can crop up. Ann aptly describes the right method of training to become a Medium, and the deep commitment this path entails.

Daphne Helliwell, B.A. (Hons) Open

About the Author

During her professional life, Ann has been involved in some very unusual and exciting situations. She studied many different levels of mediumship, and her spirit guides took her into situations that the ordinary person wouldn't even dream of exploring.

Ann developed her mediumship under the tutelage of Britain's top medium and teacher, Ivy Northage. One of the foremost colour therapists, Win Kent, taught her the psychology and therapeutics of colour healing.

Ann's book is in two parts. The largest section tells us about her personal psychic pathway and the difficulties that she encountered in the beginning. The second part teaches others how to develop their psychic ability to enhance their own lives.

Ann wants to reach out to those who experienced the same problems that she did when trying to understand their gifts, and who now wish to find their own pathway.

Even for those who do not wish to progress their own psychic nature, Ann's book will help by showing that when we die, it is only the beginning...

Contents

<< PART ONE >>

Introduction

It is time, love, to break off that sombre rose,
shut up the stars and bury the ash in the earth;
and, in the rising of the light, wake with those who awoke
or go on in the dream, reaching the other shore of the sea
which has no other shore.
Pablo Neruda

A soft yellow light chases the shadows from my room, and I can see my windows with the curtains drawn to keep out the night.

Something's disturbed my sleep, and although the light seems familiar, there is an unsettled feeling in my stomach. Trying to raise myself, a stab of fear spreads through me as I find I'm unable to move or cry out.

My eyes are drawn to movement above my head, and I see the lampshade swinging. I try to duck as it drops from the ceiling, but it shoots up again without hitting me. Everything seems to be moving, including my window. Undulating, it moves from my field of vision, then back in again.

Realisation finally hits me; I'm having an out-of-body experience, which has happened to me many times before. But it's rare for me to wake during the initial stages of my astral self detaching from my physical body. Until this process is complete, I will stay in a state of paralysis, although my astral body will continue to move around.

Now I'm feeling calmer, and the last stage of detachment is taking place. Sliding sideways from my bed, I hover in mid-air before descending slowly. Turning to an upright position, I come to a halt several inches above the floor and wait for the tilting to subside.

Now out of close range of my physical body, it's possible to move. Turning towards the bed, I recognise the sleeping figure as myself. From the top of my head snakes a long, thin cord, which connects with my astral body. A golden glow spreads from the cord, lighting my bedroom.

Gliding towards the door, it proves to be no barrier as I move through it and out onto the landing at the top of the stairs.

There is a weird silence; almost like being under water.

But my vision is sharp, and, descending into the hall, marks and shapes on the lino and carpet are intensified. Entering the kitchen, I turn towards the back door. Again I pass through the wooden frame, noting the nails and glue that hold it together.

It is the middle of summer with a full moon, and at the end of the path stands a figure by the gate. She is dressed in a long, white robe and smiles at me as I move towards her.

Reaching out, she takes my hand before rising into the air.

I'm eight years of age and she is my spirit guide. She's taking me to the astral plane, to teach me about my future work as a medium, healer and teacher.

1

A Psychic Childhood

Come away to the quiet fields
over which the great sky stretches...
And let us listen to the voice which is speaking
within us.
Jerome K. Jerome

As a child, out-of-body experiences were natural to me. Sometimes the detachments were frightening, but once clear of my physical body, I enjoyed the wonderful sensation of freedom. A soft blush of lilac light often indicated the onset of an OBE (out-of-body experience). This slowly expanded into swirling clouds of beautiful lilac mist tinged with magenta. As it filled my bedroom, my body became still, my breathing slowed and I became receptive to the colour that formed a tunnel around me. In the centre, a pinpoint of golden light widened until it engulfed me in its brilliance. The process of leaving my physical body had begun.

I still find this exquisite light astounding. There are no words to describe the luminosity of the colours, and no paint could ever do them justice. When exploring the astral plane, I didn't stray much further than the house and garden. At times I would see other astral figures, but felt I should stay away from them. My parents warned me about talking to strangers, so perhaps this rubbed off on my spirit too.

I was shy and quiet, so I found it difficult to mix with other children and I often felt isolated and alone. For some reason, I always felt different from others, without knowing why. I was lonely, so I sought comfort from books and more often than not, I could be found in the local library. I had many premonitions. These were strong, negative emotions, which I felt in my solar plexus. My stomach would twist and churn, making it impossible to think of anything other than the way I felt. I often felt sick and scared because I was sure some awful fate awaited me.

One Christmas, my brother John and I were given a new bicycle each. My parents didn't have much money to spare, so it couldn't have been easy for them to do this. However, I can still remember feeling miffed because his had straight handlebars and mine were rounded. I soon found out that I had to share my bike with my mum, who needed to use it for her work. She found the older type of handlebars easier to use, and no amount of sulking on my part got me anywhere. Despite this, I still had plenty of time to go riding, and I spent hours exploring Richmond Park and Ham Common which are lovely areas within Greater London.

One beautiful summer's day, John and I rode to the library. On the way home I became fascinated by our shadows that were being thrown against the grass verge as we cycled along, but I should have been looking where I was going. Before I knew what was happening, I had ridden into the back of a parked car, gone straight up in the air and ended up sprawled in the road. John was way in front of me by now, but on hearing my yell, he did a U-turn and pedalled back to me as fast as he could. Although my hands and knees were grazed, bleeding and full of dirt and grit from the gutter, I was more concerned about my bike and any damage to the vehicle. We checked the fender, but couldn't see any dents, nor was there a scratch on my bike. Considering the wallop that my bike had made, I was more than a bit surprised and I carefully inspected them both again. I cleaned myself as best I could and, despite my hands stinging like mad, we set off home again, but my stomach was now beginning to churn.

Stopping once more to look at my bike my thoughts kept returning to my mum. I knew I would be in trouble if it had been damaged. But no, it appeared to be all right. Neither of us mentioned the accident, but the churning feeling became stronger as time wore on.

The following day my mum used the bike for work as usual. On her way home the front wheel came off and she fell into the road. She could have been killed, but thank God, she was in a quiet side road when it happened. We found out that when I went into the back of the car, the two front forks on my bike had bent exactly level with each other so that neither of us had spotted the problem. This in turn had put pressure on the nuts and joints until the whole thing had come apart. Needless to say, I ended up in real trouble over that. As soon as the problem was over, my upset stomach returned to normal.

As I had so many OBEs, I assumed that everyone else experienced them as well, but no one ever spoke about them. On one occasion I told my mother I had been floating around the bedroom and sitting on top of the wardrobe. She gave me an intense look and didn't answer. From then on, instinct told me not to mention the OBEs again in case I was carted off to the doctor.

And I knew things. A little voice in my head would whisper that something was going to happen - and it did. I knew if someone was lying or up to something they shouldn't have been doing. This didn't just apply to other children. I was sometimes aware of adult problems. I knew instantly if a married person was having an affair, although didn't know at the time exactly what it meant. Once again, instinct told me it was something I shouldn't talk about. At times I thought it was my imagination, but if my stomach began to turn over, I just "knew" within myself that I was right.

One afternoon I was walking back from school, and felt so agitated that I dreaded going home. Mouth dry, hands clenched, I arrived to find no one in the kitchen. I called out but there was no answer. It was then I heard the moaning. I walked through the hall and stood at the bottom of the stairs, looking up. At the top, the bathroom door was ajar and I glimpsed my mother sitting on the toilet. She was crying and moaning in pain. Scared, I stood at the bottom of the stairs and yelled up to her.

"Mum what's happened? What's wrong?"

"Get your dad," she cried.

"I don't know where he is. Shall I go next door?"

She didn't answer, so I ran up the stairs and flung open the door. Sobbing and holding onto the side of the sink, she waved me away.

"Hang on. I'll go and get someone," I said, as I ran back down again.

As I reached the kitchen, the back door opened and there was my dad. He had obviously been told that something was wrong, because he ignored me and flew upstairs. I could hear their voices as he helped my mum into the bedroom. Within minutes the doctor arrived and followed in my dad's footsteps. Alone, I walked around waiting for Johnny to come home, wondering what was happening in the room above. After what seemed like an eternity, the doctor left and my father called me upstairs. Dad had lit a fire in the bedroom and mum was lying in bed looking white and tired. She patted the bedclothes as a signal for me to sit down.

"We've got something to tell you," she said.

"I was four months pregnant but I've lost the baby. You would have had another brother."

Not knowing what to say, I turned and stared into the fire.

It was then I heard a soft voice inside my head say, "He'll come back again."

This prophecy was fulfilled when, ten years later, my mother gave birth to another baby boy.

*

My interest in colour began when I was about eleven year's of age. For a long time, I had been fascinated by tiny spheres of colour that danced around my bedroom at night. These were mostly white, golden or blue. They were so vivid that it seemed as though the air in front of me had split and opened a doorway to another existence. At other times, colours appeared around people and animals. Brilliant, clear colour, shaped in swirls and circles, often floated away from the physical body, although at times darker shades intermingled with these. Apart from colours, I would repeatedly see a light grey mist shimmering around someone's head and shoulders. This mist also flowed from healthy trees, plants and flowers, but if the flowers were picked, the mist would gradually fade as they began to die.

One of my favourite hobbies was collecting beads, crystals and semi-precious gemstones and trading them with my friend Carol. Many of these were only made of glass, but I loved holding them up to the light, watching them shimmer and sparkle. Playing marbles was another game I enjoyed. Although to be truthful, I loved the colours within the marbles more than the actual game. My interest in this field developed alongside my psychic ability, and in later years I was to use them together in my readings and healing.

By the time I entered my teens I realised I was possibly the only one out of my friends who had these experiences, so I felt even more alone. Unable to tell anyone what was happening, and not wanting to be different, I bottled up my feelings inside. I made a conscious effort to prevent the OBEs from happening, and when the coloured lights appeared, I hid my head under the bedclothes. In this way I managed to control most of the astral travel, but I soon found other psychic phenomena taking its place.

When speaking to someone, faces often appeared in my mind. If I ignored them they would sometimes disappear of their own accord. At other times, it would take a conscious effort on my part to get them to leave. I did this by thinking of some mundane job I had to do. Premonitions affected me the most. They were strong, negative emotions that dried my mouth and churned my stomach. I would be filled with nervous energy, but unable to concentrate on anything until the premonition passed. Usually it would take a few hours, but at times it would last for days or weeks. It was often possible to pinpoint the source of the problem by seeing pictures in my mind, or by simply "knowing" what was about to happen. Sometimes the outcome was a complete mystery to me, and the impressions then dispersed as quickly as they came.

Despite these experiences most of the time my life was fairly normal, with only intermittent psychic activity. However, my increasing sensitivity combined with adolescence, caused me to become very emotional. I often had the overwhelming feeling that I didn't belong in this world. I was aware that something important was missing from my life, but I didn't know what. Even when I was happy, this feeling would sometimes take me by surprise. Needless to say, I kept this information to myself.

2
I Meet a Fellow Psychic

After I married and had children, my life became more settled. Nevertheless, although I loved my two girls, I wasn't happy in my marriage. Looking back, I must have married Tom to escape from a lonely life. As the problem was within me, I found I had only exchanged my old situation for a similar one. Knowing I couldn't walk away from my responsibilities as a mother, I was determined to make our marriage work, so I channelled all my energy into my family.

At first, Tom and I lived with my parents in their flat at Kingston in Surrey, but after a few weeks we moved to a large Victorian house in nearby Surbiton, where we rented the ground floor. Apart from having another door added to the house for the tenants who lived upstairs, no alterations had been made. The ground floor had a long, narrow hall that ran the length of the house. All the rooms, with the exception of the kitchen, lead off from it. There was no bathroom, but we did have a separate toilet for ourselves. It was impossible for two people to get in the kitchen at the same time, but we loved it, as it was our own home. The garden was long, narrow and divided into two. One half was ours and the other belonged to the people living upstairs. On our side was a lawn surrounded by flowers, but our neighbours had turned their half into a vegetable plot.

One hot summer's day, Tom and I decided to go out. Shirley from upstairs called out to us as we were leaving.

"Are you going to be out all day?" she called.

"Probably," I answered. "Why?"

"We're not going anywhere so we'll keep an eye on your place for you."

"Oh. Okay, thanks," I said. "See you later then."

"What's come over her?" Tom asked. "Normally she never has two words to say to us."

We had been driving for about ten minutes when I had the overwhelming urge to go back home.

"Something's wrong," I told Tom, "I don't know what it is but I've got to check that everything's all right."

As we walked through the back gate, we took our neighbours completely by surprise. They were on our lawn sunbathing, surrounded by a picnic.

They didn't know what to do. They began collecting up the dishes but we told them to stay put. After checking the flat, we realised the only "problem" that had existed was our upstairs neighbours and their picnic. To the best of our knowledge, they didn't take advantage again, but neither did they offer us any of their homegrown vegetables!

We had been living in the Surbiton house for five years when the opportunity arose to buy a semi-detached house only a few streets away. Fed up with having to return to my parents to have a bath, we jumped at the chance of moving to a house with a bathroom, and my parents kindly loaned us the money for the deposit.

The young couple that sold the house to us were in the process of a divorce. After we moved in we then found out that the people who had sold the house to them were also divorced. The atmosphere was a bit depressing and I hoped that it was not an omen. Determined that it was not going to happen to us, I quickly made the place cheerful with new curtains and bright colours on the walls.

We had been living there for a few months when the adjoining house was put up for sale. Bob and Julie, the new neighbours, were young like us with two children about the same age as ours. We quickly became firm friends and I found that I shared the same interests as Julie in music, reading and art. She was also psychic, and it was through her that my path of destiny decided it was time to get serious.

"I've always wanted to find out more about the subject," she told me. "But I didn't know anyone who had experiences similar to mine, nor did I have a clue where to begin looking."

At last, I had found a soul mate with whom I could share my bottled up emotions concerning my psychic nature. Julie said that now that we were together, we should be able to do something about it. She also said that she found the subject a bit scary. By this time I had also confided in Julie about more personal matters, including the state of my marriage. So far, things hadn't changed, but knowing I could turn to her helped me to cope during a difficult period in my life.

We talked for ages about psychic matters, despite not knowing much about the subject. Our ignorance showed when we experimented with the alphabet and tumbler method of trying to contact spirits. This procedure was often used as an alternative to the Ouija board. Once the letters were cut out and placed around the edge of the table, there was room for the glass to move. It would have been more difficult on a smaller board to see which letters were being pointed out.

One evening, Julie and I went into my dining room to see if we could contact spirit in this way. I had already cut out the square pieces of paper, drawn a letter on each and placed them in a large circle on the table. I added two more with the words "yes" on one, and "no" on the other. The glass tumbler was placed upside down in the centre of the circle, and we had a pen and notepaper ready for any messages. Sitting opposite each other we placed our index fingers lightly on the bottom of the tumbler.

Looking intently at the glass, Julie asked, "Is anybody there?"

Nothing happened.

We glanced at each other and I then repeated, "Is anybody there?"

This time the glass began to move slowly around the table until it stopped in front of the word "yes."

"Who are you?"

My arm began to tingle and the sensation spread through my hand and into my finger.

"I'm sure it's going to move again," I said.

The tumbler circled the table, gathering speed until it came to a halt in front of the square with "no" written on it. It then moved around each letter spelling out the word "body."

Julie looked at me. "It doesn't make sense. Ask again?"

Glancing at the table I asked, "You must be someone. Can you tell us your name?"

Again, nothing happened. No feeling in my arm. No movement from the glass. Looking at each other, we raised our eyebrows before Julie once more repeated the question. Simultaneously, my arm tingled as the tumbler moved. It gathered speed, spinning around the circle so fast we had difficulty keeping our fingers on it. Finally it slowed and began to spell out a message. Julie was writing the letters down as the tumbler stopped in front of each one, before coming to a halt. The message read, "Ann divorce – marry Peter C."

"Well, I guess the divorce part may well come true," I told her, "but I don't know anyone called Peter."

As I finished speaking, an awful screeching noise came from the wall by the table. Scared stiff we ran into the hall. We waited for a few minutes, but as the noise didn't come again, we tentatively walked back into the room. Too unnerved to continue, we packed everything away.

The following morning Julie told me that Bob had been standing at the other side of the wall, blowing into a comb covered with tissue paper. He was hoping to frighten us and he well and truly succeeded. Childish though it was, he scared the living daylights out of us both.

Several years passed before we were to remember the message and how we were protected by our spirit guides from negative forces.

3

Another Psychic Neighbour

Opportunity
They do me wrong who say I come no more,
When once I knock and fail to find you in.
For every day I stand outside your door:
And bid you wake, and rise to fight and win.
Wail not for precious chances passed away.
Weep not for golden ages on the wane.
Each night I burn the records of the day:
At sunrise every soul is born again.
Walter Malone

Over the following months my marriage deteriorated. When I suggested to Tom that we both had counselling, he flatly refused and whenever I tried to discuss the way I felt, he turned away. One afternoon he walked up behind me as I stood looking out the window with tears running down my face.

"What's the matter with you? What are you crying for?"

"I don't know. I only know that I'm miserable," I said, turning and moving away from him.

Knowing I couldn't live this way any longer and that it was time I did something about it, I asked my parents if the girls and I could stay with them for a while. I thought that some time apart might help us both to sort out our feelings. Reluctantly, Tom agreed. He was hoping it wouldn't be long before we were back together.

During the three months we were with my parents, Tom saw Karen and Nicky whenever he wanted, but he kept pestering me to come home. Although I knew I couldn't stay with my parents for much longer, I didn't want to go back. Yet, the children and I had nowhere else to go, so I agreed to try again. Nothing changed and soon our lives were the same as before. We grew further and further apart over the next two years and then we decided to separate. I moved with the girls to my parent's house in Hampton. This meant a long drive back and forth to Surbiton each day, so the girls could stay at the same schools. While the divorce was going through, Tom lived in our house until it was sold. We divided everything we owned between us. There wasn't enough money for me to buy another property, so my children and I ended up as another statistic on the housing list.

Before I became eligible for a council house, I was placed in what is known as "half-way housing." This consisted of one very large room, plus a tiny kitchen on the top floor of a three-story house in Surbiton. There wasn't a bedroom, so I divided the larger room with a curtain to conceal the beds. Knowing we would probably spend some months living there, my dad and I cleaned and painted to make it fairly habitable.

Soon after this, a woman from the housing department came to see me, and she nearly exploded when she saw what we had done.

"What on earth do you think you're doing?" she spluttered. "If you make these rooms too comfortable, the next family to move in won't want to move out again. Plus, you've been given the best rooms in the house as you're a single parent."

"If that's the case," I said, "I dread to think what the other rooms are like. There is no way I would let my children live in such filthy conditions. And I doubt very much if you would set one foot in here unless you had to."

Without another word she turned on her heel and stomped off down the stairs. The Council representative never mentioned the decorating again, but she still checked on me once a week to make sure that I was toeing the line.

There was one other family living on my floor and shortly after we moved in, there was a knock on my door. Standing before me was a small, slightly built Asian man with intense brown eyes. He introduced himself as Kishore and then pointed across the landing, saying he lived there with his wife Shanta and his young family.

He said, "As you are living on your own, please call on us if you need any help."

"Thanks. That's kind of you. But I'm sure it won't come to that."

Looking at me intently he said, "I hope you're right, but you can't be too careful with some of the people living here." He then followed this with, "You have a gold ring with a large, yellow stone. It's tucked away at the back of a drawer. You must take it out and wear it because it's lucky for you, especially where money is concerned."

Before I could answer, his door opened and a beautiful woman dressed in a sari came over to us. This was Shanta, and she asked me over for tea.

Although their kitchen was larger than mine, their living area was only half the size. Mattresses took up two thirds of the floor, so there was little room for anything else. Over tea, Kishore told me that he and the family had arrived a few months earlier from India, in the hopes of a better life in England. The area where they lived was very poor, and it had taken him a long time to save money for the fare. He and Shanta were hoping to be given permanent Council accommodation. Despite the way they were living, they appeared to be happy. When I returned to my room, I realised just how lucky I was to have the better living accommodation.

Before going to bed that night, I remembered what he had said about my ring. It was true: I did have a ring like the one he described. But how on earth did he know about it? What's more – how did he find out I was living alone with my children? Going to my dressing table, I pulled out the drawer and rummaged through it for my ring. Just as he said, it was tucked away at the back. I took it out and placed it on my finger, certain there wasn't any way he could have known about it.

The next time I saw Kishore, he said, "You're lonely, but you will soon be involved in another relationship and despite how you're feeling now, you will get married again."

Staring at him, I asked, "How on earth do you know all this?"

"I have a lady in spirit called a Goddess," he told me "she tells me these things about you."

Feeling apprehensive, I asked, "What on earth do you mean?"

"She's in my head. I speak to her and she looks after me. In India I had many people who came to seek guidance from my Goddess. She would advise them on what to do. She knows you need help and she's telling me this about you."

"Well, your Goddess is wrong about the marriage, as I've no intention of ever getting married again."

"In time you'll change your mind. She says you will work all over the world helping people in the same way as myself."

I gave a short laugh. "That's rubbish. I don't know what you're talking about."

He smiled. "Ah, you will find out soon enough," he said as he turned and walked back into his room.

Kishore and Shanta did look out for me though, without interfering in my life. He gave me other messages, and despite finding it difficult to believe what he told me, I learnt to accept these with the same goodwill in which they were given.

Just as Kishore had said, I began another relationship with someone I met through Julie. On telling Kishore about this, he answered, "Don't let yourself become too close to this man, because this love affair will end. He's not for you, and you'll get hurt."

Despite being aware from the start that our romance wasn't going anywhere, I still became deeply involved. After some time we both decided to end it and I was left feeling pretty miserable.

Within days of us splitting up, Kishore came to see me. "I know how sad you are, but it will pass in time. I told you this man wasn't the one for you."

"If our relationship wasn't meant to be, why did I have to be involved at all? What's more, how the hell did you know that he had gone? Have you been listening at my door?" I asked in exasperation.

Speaking quietly he told me, "The only way you're going to understand how other people feel is for you to experience it yourself. Your unhappiness is necessary for your psychic and spiritual growth, although you cannot understand that yet."

"There's no way that I'm going through other situations like this, Kishore, because I'm not going to be doing the work you keep talking about. I know you were right about this relationship, but quite honestly anyone could have guessed that I would have met someone else and that it could have ended. And it's pretty obvious I would feel unhappy about it." Before he could reply, I opened the door and gestured for him to leave, saying that I had other things to do.

It wasn't long before Kishore was back again. He said, "Knowing how depressed you've been, I thought I should make you a prayer bracelet." He showed me a length of black wool, which was knotted in several places. "I spent yesterday praying with my Goddess, and each knot represents a prayer. It's very special and will help you if you wear it. Do not remove it though. It must be worn at all times until it disintegrates."

Taking it from him, I apologised for the way I had spoken to him before.

"There's no need for apologies. I am your friend. Now, let me tie this around your wrist."

Thanking him for all the trouble he had gone to, I held out my hand so that he could secure the woollen braid.

After a week of wearing the bracelet, it began to irritate me. It was always getting wet, so it wasn't long before my wrist became sore. I had to take it off. I cut it into pieces, put it into a bag and wrapped it in newspaper. After dark, I put it in one of the dustbins at the back of the building. I thought I could keep this from Kishore, as most of the time I wore long sleeves.

Imagine how I felt when he confronted me the very next day, with the bag and wool I had so carefully discarded the previous night.

Flushed with embarrassment I looked at him without speaking.

"Why did you do it?" he asked.

Tetchily, I said, "You seem to know so much about my life, so why don't you tell me."

"I don't know why you took it off, only that you had - and I was shown where to find it."

"Are you telling me that you actually went through that dustbin to prove your Goddess was right?"

"It was necessary. The prayers were to protect and help you and this now has to be burnt."

"Look Kishore, I appreciate you doing these things for me, but I can't wear wool around my wrist because it gets wet and makes me sore."

"I understand," he said quietly, as he turned and walked away.

Several days later he approached me again. "Would you wear this? I have made it large enough for you to put around your waist."

In his hand was a replica of the black, woollen bracelet, only this time in a much larger size.

"How long have you spent praying over this?" I asked.

"Two days," he replied.

"You don't give up easily, do you?"

He shook his head.

"Thanks Kishore, it's worth another try," I said, taking it from him.

Happy again, he said, "You won't be sorry."

I put the prayer belt on under my clothes, and thinking of how much he was trying to help me, I simply put up with it getting wet when I bathed.

*

Living on the floor below mine, was a married man with children. Whenever he saw me he told me how much he fancied me. He wouldn't take no for an answer, so he really began to get on my nerves. One day when I was walking up the stairs, I met him on his way down, and once more he fed me the same old story.

"If you don't leave me alone, I'll tell your wife what you're up to."

"Really," he said, "you're friendly with that Indian lot, but too stuck up for me."

"Being friendly is one thing but that's not what you're after," I said pushing past him.

"Snotty bitch," I heard him remark as I reached the top of the stairs.

About a week later, after shopping, I discovered I had lost my purse. There wasn't much money in it, but what little I had was needed.

That same evening I opened the door to find the creep from downstairs, with my purse in his hands.

"Is this yours? It's got your name inside."

"Yes it is. Where did you find it?"

"It was lying on the stairs."

Hovering by the door, he watched as I opened it. The money had gone but all my odd bits of paper, plus a couple of photographs were still there.

"There was money in here as well."

"Not when I found it," he said looking me straight in the eyes. "I don't suppose you're going to ask me in for a coffee for bringing it back then."

"You suppose right," I answered, closing the door in his face.

On seeing Kishore the next day he asked, "Have you lost your purse?"

"Yes, but I've got it back now." I then told him what had happened.

"It's obvious that he took the money to spite me," I said, but I know I'd never be able to prove it."

"No. You're right. You'll have to forget it," he replied.

It wasn't until I was getting into bed that night, that I realised I hadn't been wearing my ring.

*

When we first moved into the halfway house, the council said that tenants couldn't keep pets in their rooms. At that time I had a white Persian cat called Topaz and I had no intention of giving her away. If I knew the woman from the council was coming, I turned the television on, put the cat in a basket and placed her under the bed. I would then speak to the woman in the kitchen while the girls stayed in the other room. We hadn't told anyone in the building about her, not even Kishore and Shanta, as we didn't want to risk having her taken away from us. Whenever I disposed of Topaz's food cans, I always wrapped them up in newspaper before throwing them away in the bins.

One evening soon after the incident with my purse, the guy from downstairs called on me again. He was holding something behind his back, and looked over his shoulder furtively before asking if he could come in, but I refused.

Looking behind him again at Kishore's door, he whispered that he had something to show me. He held up an empty can that once held cat food. "I told you about the kind of people you mix with," he whispered. "They've been putting cat food in their curries."

"Don't be stupid. It must belong to someone who has a cat."

"Animals aren't allowed here, except for them of course. It's the kind of thing they'd eat."

"Where did you find the can?"

"Downstairs, in the bin," he answered, with a smug grin on his face.

"Were there anymore where that came from?"

"No. I only found this one. The bin was too bloody dirty for me to search for others."

"Just what were you doing rummaging through the bins in the first place?" I asked more loudly.

"Sssh, keep your voice down," he said. "I threw something away by mistake so I had to look," he said, staring down at the floor.

"Yeah, I'm sure you did. Go away and leave me alone."

With that I closed the door and leaned against it. As his footsteps became fainter, I began to giggle. I told the girls what he had said, and before long we fell about laughing.

Tomorrow, I thought, I'll have to come clean to Kishore and Shanta about Topaz, and I'll have to warn them about that guy, just in case he decides to cause them trouble. After telling them what had happened, they smiled and said they had known about the cat for sometime.

"Don't tell me – it was your Goddess who told you about her, wasn't it?"

"No, it wasn't. Sometimes we can hear her crying through the wall when you go out, even though you leave the radio on."

They promised not to say anything to anyone else about our cat. As for the young guy from downstairs – they said he was an ignorant racist. As time went by I learnt to trust the predictions that Kishore made, even though I still could not see myself doing the work he had predicted.

Julie and I were often invited to try the delicious Indian food that Shanta spent most of the day cooking. They told us about India. How poor the country was. How even the basic needs which we take for granted, were denied them. Kishore knew England could offer his children a good education and a better way of life. He told me, "Once you've moved and are settled, you'll meet your future husband. There will never be anyone else in your life, and you'll eventually work together along your psychic pathway." He had been right about so many things, and although I still had doubts about working in the same way as him, I didn't express them.

We had been living in the halfway house for six months when I was offered a maisonette in a housing complex overlooking playing fields. It was close to both schools that the girls were already attending, so there would be little disruption in their lives. Kishore and Shanta had been re-housed in another town, and although we were still in contact with each other, it was difficult to meet up, as neither of us had any transport.

After I had moved, a close friend in the police often called on me if he was in my area. He came to see me one evening, bringing a colleague along with him. The name of his friend was Peter Caulfield and two years later we were married.

*

A few weeks after our wedding, Julie and I remembered the message given to us after we had used the alphabet method for contacting spirit. When we told Pete, at first he didn't believe us. As a policeman, logic told him that this kind of thing didn't happen. He became more interested when I told him about the psychic messages Kishore had given me, but like me, he couldn't see himself becoming involved in psychic work. Despite being sceptical, he did agree one night to my suggestion that we could try to make contact with spirit. So, once more the alphabet was laid out in a circle with a tumbler placed in the centre.

We turned the lights down and sat opposite each other, with the pen and notepaper by my side for messages. I asked the usual question "Is anybody there?" Pete was trying to keep a straight face, but I could feel my finger and arm beginning to tingle.

"Don't laugh Pete – it's going to move."

Slowly the glass slid across the table and came to a stop in front of the letter G.

"You're pushing it," said Peter.

"No I'm not," I replied, taking my finger off the glass. "Look, how can I push it with just the tip of my finger?" I replaced my finger on the bottom of the tumbler. Once again came the old familiar tingle and the tumbler moved across the table to stop in front of the letter O.

"It feels cold in here," Pete said, as the glass began to pick up speed.

Nodding in reply, I found I was having a job to keep my finger on the glass and watch out for the messages at the same time.

Finally the tumbler came to a halt after spelling out the words, "Go away."

The look of surprise on Pete's face told me he wasn't that doubtful any more.

"Why should we go away?" he asked quietly.

Immediately the tumbler moved quickly from letter to letter. It was impossible for me to keep my finger on it any longer and Pete was now standing up, trying to do the same. We sat back helplessly, as the glass sped along spelling out the same message, over and over again. Then suddenly, it shot off the end of the table and smashed against the wall.

Now thoroughly frightened, I was aware of how cold the room had become. I could see that Pete was nervous too, so he sprung up to put on the lights.

"Come on Ann. Let's go. It doesn't feel right in here."

My mouth was dry as I said, "Okay. We can clear this up in the morning; but I'm leaving all the lights on tonight."

Closing the door firmly behind us, we made our way to bed. Snuggling up to Pete I asked, "Are you still sceptical?"

"No way," was his reply.

Neither of us felt nervous the following morning as we entered the living room in broad daylight. The temperature was back to normal, and I vowed never again to use that method of contacting spirit.

4

The Path Begins to Appear

After several months of financial struggle, Peter and I saved enough money to buy our own home. Our house was a three-story town house in Kingston. Although we had been happy in our council house, our new home was much larger and it was close to the river and to Richmond Park. We could have as many pets as we wanted, without the hassle of someone checking up on us. Shortly after moving we decided to buy another cat. Julie had told me about a woman in London who bred Siamese kittens and I arranged to drive over one evening with Nicky to buy one.

The night before, I had gone to bed feeling very uneasy, and was sure it was connected to our journey the following evening. In the early hours of the morning, I awoke with a vivid picture in my mind of Nicky and me in a car crash. What I saw was so real and three dimensional, that I could feel the shock of the accident vibrating through my body. Feeling queasy, I made my way to the bathroom and splashed my face with cold water. When I felt better, I went downstairs to the kitchen and made myself tea. As I sat there, trying to get the image of the crash out of my mind, I could not shake off the feeling of impending doom. Before long, Nicky came downstairs, dressed and ready for school. Over breakfast I told her about my psychic dream and that I thought it would be best to cancel the trip that evening.

Pushing herself away from the table, she said, "Oh mum, I've been looking forward to this all week."

"I know you're upset, love, but I'm so sure we're going to have an accident that it's not worth taking the risk."

"How do you know it wasn't just a dream?"

"It was too real to be a dream, but I'll think about it and if I feel better by the time you come out of school, we'll still go."

During the day the uneasiness persisted, but it became weaker as the day wore on, and when I collected Nicky I could see the look of hope on her face as she got into the car.

"Okay, the trip's still on, but you're going to have to wear your seat belt, as I'm not taking any chances." (This was in the days when wearing a seat belt was optional rather than a legal requirement.)

Nicky flung her arms around my neck and gave me a big kiss.

Before we began our journey that evening, I made sure both belts were secure. Driving at a moderate speed, I kept a watchful eye on the rush-hour traffic and tried to be prepared for any emergency. I made my way into a filter lane for a left-hand turn. On my right, the line of traffic was at a standstill, but I was in second gear, moving slowly behind the vehicle in front. A huge, white truck blocked my view to my right, but unknown to me, the driver had left enough space for a car to turn in front of it. A vehicle with three young women inside had driven from the opposite direction, and the driver wanted to turn into a side road on my left. Stupidly, the person in the truck beckoned the driver to go through the gap in front, despite the fact that our lane was moving. The car drove straight into us, pushing my car over the pavement and into a garden before coming to a halt against the wall of the house behind it. Nicky was flung forward, hitting her head on the windscreen, and I caught the steering wheel in my stomach. If we hadn't been wearing seat belts, we could have ended up with more than mere bruises. My car was badly damaged, and the police had to push it out of the garden and around the corner to keep the traffic moving. The police pulled the man and the girls over for questioning, and then the police drove us home. By the time Pete arrived home, I felt as shocked as I had the night before. I was still shaking as I told him the whole story.

"It was the strongest premonition I've ever had, and I knew we should have stayed at home".

"You weren't to know for sure that it was going to happen tonight, it could have happened anytime. You can't stay in forever, just in case there is an accident. At least you had the sense to wear belts. The important thing is that neither of you were badly hurt," Pete said.

"Mmm, you are right. However, I think these premonitions are getting out of hand now. Although they're warnings of some kind, they're not always clear, and I don't know what to do about them."

*

My old friend and ex-neighbour, Julie, was in the process of a divorce and had to attend a hearing in court in connection with custody of her children. There was some acrimony over this, and she had asked me to be a character witness, along with Phyllis Smith, the headmistress of her children's school. The hearing had already been set for the week following my accident. As I had no transport, I had to work out how to get there by bus. This wasn't difficult, but when I arrived I found Julie had already gone in, while Phyllis was sitting outside on her own. I had met Phyllis when my own children attended her school, but I didn't know her well. I thought it was good of her to give up her time for the hearing as she had a long way to travel.

Still breathing heavily from walking fast, I greeted her as I sat down.

"It's all right Ann, they won't be calling us in just yet, so you've time to get your breath back," she said smiling.

"Thank goodness for that. I thought I was going to be late, I'm not used to travelling on buses these days."

"Do you normally drive then?" she asked.

"Yes, but my car is off the road as I was involved in an awful accident last week."

"What on earth happened?"

I told her about the accident and she asked if anyone had been hurt.

"No, thank God, but if I'd been driving any faster, I might not have been here today."

For some reason, I then felt compelled to tell her my story about my premonition. She listened and said, "You must realise that you are mediumistic."

"What do you mean?" I asked.

"Well, it's obvious to me that you're very psychic and that someone in spirit was trying to warn you.'

Surprised at this, I asked, "Do you believe in all that psychic stuff then?"

"Oh yes. Ever since my parents died several years ago, I've visited a medium to make contact with them."

I then asked Phyllis, "If I wanted to find out more about this, what do you think I should do?"

"Well, you could always come along with me. I'll let you know when I'm going to make my next appointment."

"Do you mind if I think about it first and discuss it with Pete?" I asked.

"No, of course I don't. I won't ask you anything else about yourself, because the less I know about you the better."

"Why's that," I asked.

"It's so that I can't pass on any information about you. That makes it easier for her to give you a reading."

Phyllis gave me her telephone number, and then Julie came out and told us that we wouldn't be needed, as she was awarded custody anyway.

*

Over dinner I recounted my conversation with Phyllis, and asked Pete what he thought about it.

"Well, it's obvious you need to get something done about this. It has affected you all your life and it doesn't look as if it's going away. If anything, it seems to be getting stronger."

"Mmm. You have to be pretty clever to be a headmistress of a school. So, Phyllis should know what she's talking about. Anyway, I've got nothing to lose so I may as well give it a try."

*

Phyllis came for me and drove me to Twickenham to meet Muriel Miller. On the way she explained that Mrs. Miller was a trance medium, which meant that she was taken over by spirits who would then speak through her. I found all of this difficult to believe but I decided to try and keep an open mind. We soon pulled up outside a small, terraced house that had white net curtains at the windows, and a small, neat front garden.

Mrs. Miller was an elderly lady, and although small in stature she exuded so much energy we had to walk quickly to keep up with her. Ushering us into a small room that was crowded with furniture, she asked if we would like a cup of tea to help relax us both before our readings. We hadn't quite finished before she was back again to lead us upstairs to her sanctuary. Expecting to be shown into a special room set out with religious artefacts, I was surprised to be shown into a small bedroom, containing a single bed, a chest of drawers and a wardrobe.

The medium asked us both to sit on the bed while she made herself comfortable in the only chair. As Muriel closed her eyes, Phyllis silently handed me her notebook and pen so that I could write down the messages for her. After a sigh, Muriel began to pray. We both said amen when she did. Then still keeping her eyes closed, she turned her head towards

Phyllis. Her voice became childish, as she introduced herself
as Topsy, Mrs. Miller's young Cockney guide. Phyllis
immediately recognised the voice and greeted Topsy warmly.
Topsy then went on to give Phyllis personal details about her
life. As I watched the medium's face and listened to this
voice coming from her, I had the urge to laugh. Surely this
was a con. How could Phyllis believe it?

Topsy said goodbye, and Mrs. Miller sat quietly for a
moment or two. Then turning her head towards me she said,
"I'll come to you soon, although you don't believe what you
are hearing." Taken by surprise, I had a strong impression of
someone looking out at me from behind her closed eyes.

Turning her head back towards Phyllis, she began to
speak in a deeper voice. The voice claimed to be Phyllis's
father. Phyllis was overcome with emotion as Muriel reached
out to hold her hand. Her father gave details of his life before
he passed over, in addition to personal information about
Phyllis that had not been covered in previous visits.

Then it was my turn. As I handed Phyllis the notebook,
a soft gentle voice with a distinct Spanish accent addressed
me. "Welcome, my child. I am Sister Anna, your doorkeeper.
I have been with you since you were born to this world, and
at last I can speak to you face to face."

"You have difficulty believing, and we do understand.
You have experienced many problems in your life, but these
have been necessary for your own development. Now the
time has arrived for you to develop your spiritual and psychic
knowledge further."

Once again I was receiving the same message that
Kishore had given me. "I've been told this before, but I know
very little about mediumship, and I've no idea how to begin."

"You will be guided by us, child, as you have been all
your life. This time next year your work will take you
throughout the British Isles, and once your husband has the
proof he seeks, he will join you."

Sister Anna then gave me personal details about my life. She was so accurate that I knew she could not have gleaned information from Phyllis, because Phyllis knew so little about me. Our readings lasted two hours, and as we were leaving, Mrs. Miller turned to me and said, "It's important to find a good developing circle, so you should begin your search for the truth in the Spiritualist churches."

Thanking her, we said goodbye. As Phyllis started the car, she asked me what I thought.

"At first I thought she was making it all up but she certainly knew an awful lot about my life. I have a lot of questions that need answers. I think I'll take her advice and visit the Spiritualist churches to see how other mediums work. Then I'll see where it leads me."

After she dropped me off at home, I went over the messages again. I was still unsure. Was there some way Mrs. Miller had read my mind? The only way I would find out was to do as she advised. So, I fished out the telephone book and looked up the address of Kingston Spiritualist church.

*

My car was repaired and back in time for me to drive to the church one day the following week, for an afternoon of clairvoyance with a medium called Beryl Cartmell. Once inside, I could see that the church was far larger than I had thought, and was set out with rows of chairs in front of a raised platform. Several people were already seated, despite having another half hour to go before the meeting started. As I made my way to the back, other people quickly followed me in until the hall was filled. Looking around me, I could see that most of the people were either middle aged or elderly. There seemed to be only a sprinkling of younger people over the age of twenty. I was struck by the normality of it all. No one was wearing a black cloak or a pointy hat, and I could just as well have been at a meeting of the Women's Institute.

There were two chairs on the platform. Soon, a woman of about sixty climbed up to the platform and sat down. She was followed by a well-built, younger lady, who sat in the other chair, briefly looking out at us before closing her eyes. The doors were closed and an expectant hush fell over the hall.

The first lady stood up and said she was the chairperson for the afternoon. Turning to the other woman, she introduced her as the medium Beryl Cartmell. Beryl walked to the front of the platform where she opened the service with a prayer. She followed this by pacing back and forth with her head cocked to one side as though she was listening to someone. Abruptly she turned, and pointing her finger at someone in the congregation, she said, "I want to come to the lady sitting in the middle row, nearer this end - the lady wearing glasses and a beige sweater." The woman in question was pointing at herself, and Beryl nodding said, "Yes, you my love." Several heads turned to see who the lucky recipient could be, as a small woman of about forty years of age hesitantly raised her hand.

Beryl Cartmell said, "Just call out a clear yes or no, dear. The vibration of your voice will make the communication from spirit stronger." She turned back once more, again cocking her head to one side.

"I have a slim man here with me. He is about six feet in height, slightly stooped, with thinning, grey hair. He is clean-shaven, but once had a beard. He tells me he passed over with cancer a few years ago." She listened again before saying, "It was cancer of the lungs, and I want to say that this man was your father. Can you take this at all?"

"Thank you, yes I can," replied the woman.

"He's telling me that your mother is ill, and you have been very worried about her. She will pull through. It isn't her time yet to pass over."

"Yes, that's right," was the answer.

"You need to have a break yourself, he says, otherwise you'll end up being ill as well. Now I have the name of Bert. Can you take that name in connection with him?"

"That's his name," the woman answered.

Beryl ended the message, and then working quickly, made her way around the room for the next hour and a half.

She didn't come to me, but I was impressed. She didn't ask any direct questions, and although her messages were short, they seemed fairly accurate. When she finished her clairvoyance she closed down the meeting in prayer and everyone filed out of the hall.

*

When I got home, I told Pete about my experiences, and although he was interested in everything I told him, he was still reluctant to come with me on other occasions, so I either went alone or with Julie.

Some of the mediums I saw were awful, fishing for information, asking questions and sometimes giving out messages that couldn't be accepted, no matter how they wrapped them up. Others were excellent, and I had several messages myself from relatives who had died and wanted to grasp the opportunity to show me they still lived on. Time and again, I was told I should be working. On several occasions I was introduced to spiritual guides who said they were waiting for me to develop in a circle. Then one afternoon I saw a medium named Larry Bell.

"You should be up here, on this platform doing the same as me," he said.

Although the information he gave was the same as I had had so many times before, I was not too impressed with Larry Bell. He had the gift of the gab and he seemed very confident in what he said, but he seemed to work more on a predictive level, rather than bringing through departed spirits. Despite this, I thought that Pete might want to come with me the next time Larry was appearing. Most mediums tended to be women, and it made a change to see a man working a little bit differently. Agreeing to my suggestion, we both turned up one afternoon at a Spiritualist church in Tolworth to see Larry in action. He had given several messages to others, but just before the end of the session he came to Pete.

"I'm an ex-copper," he said to Pete. "And so are you." He then followed this with the number Pete held when he was in the force, plus other personal details. We thought that this was impressive, so when the session was over, I asked Larry if he knew where I could find a circle or class to develop my mediumship.

"Now listen to me, love. You don't need to go with anyone else, because you can do this by yourself. Find somewhere quiet to sit, and keep asking spirits to show themselves to you. Write down what you feel they are trying to say. Always ask for information that you can check out. You only need a little bit of polishing around the edges anyway – just to build your confidence." We chatted a while longer, and although I felt a bit unsure of doing this on my own rather than in a circle, I thought that maybe this was the way spirit wanted me to learn.

5

The Wrong Road to Development

Sitting quietly in my spare bedroom, I asked over and over again in my mind, for spirit to show me something. It wasn't easy trying to relax and keep my mind free of everyday thoughts. After a few minutes a picture formed. The image was of my brother John and his wife Jennifer. He was shown with his head shaven and sitting in a wheelchair. His wife was slowly pushing him along a winding drive towards a huge building, which I instinctively knew was a hospital. John had recently been diagnosed with multiple sclerosis and I was shocked to see this image of him so disabled. However, I understood I was seeing something that could happen in the future. Pulling my note-pad towards me, I wrote the date and details of the vision down. I thought about the long, winding drive and why Jen was walking so slowly. I came to the conclusion that it was symbolic of the journey ahead of them. I blinked back tears as strong feelings of sadness and hopelessness engulfed me. Unable to continue, I put the notebook away, left the room and concentrated on mundane chores to take my mind off what I had seen.

Night after night, I would sit for a short while to see if I could receive clairvoyance. At times, I perceived snippets of things happening in my family. Sometimes they were connected with problems that I was already aware of, so I dismissed them as imagination. Despite this, I still wrote down all the information so that I could check it at a later date. After doing this for two or three weeks, I began to feel nervous each time I entered the room. One evening, I heard the flapping of wings, and something flew past my head and out through the corner of the wall. Unsettled, I thought that watching television would take my mind off the psychic scene for a while. As I entered the living room I saw several faces suspended in the air. Life-sized, they appeared to be made out of a white mist, and each one was contorted in some way. One had his mouth wide open in a scream, whilst the others were twisted in pain. Transfixed by this scene of horror, I forced myself to move slowly backwards into the kitchen. As I did this they began to disperse. I was so shaken by what I had seen that as I made myself some tea I kept looking over my shoulder, certain they were going to reappear again. I carried the tea into the living room and turned on the television, but was still too unsettled to take anything in. Turning it off, I went back to the kitchen. As I rinsed my cup, I had the distinct impression that someone was behind me. Whipping round quickly, I envisaged seeing another face – or worse still – some awful figure following me. I was relieved to find I was alone.

By this time my stomach was churning and a sensation of pins and needles was creeping up and down my spine. Pete was working late, so with a strong urge to forget everything that had happened, I decided on an early night. Walking up the stairs, the feeling still clung to me that something or someone was invading my space. I got ready for bed very quickly and I climbed between the sheets, pulled up the covers and turned off the light. Despite the darkness, I could see a huge ball of grey mist over my bed. Before I could take it in, our double bed was somehow lifted clear off the floor. "Oh my God," I screamed, as I lunged for the light. Immediately the bed was dropped and the mist and uneasy feelings vanished. Enough is enough, I thought. There is no way I'm going to carry on like this on my own. Thinking about the way the bed was lifted, scared me half to death. I realised it dropped as I screamed "God". In someway I was attracting the wrong type of spirit to me, and that was one road I was not prepared to go down.

Pete came home a few hours later, to find all the house lights on and me sitting up in bed reading. As he listened, it was obvious he was now as worried as me. Turning out the lights in the early hours of the morning, we half expected something else to happen, but it didn't, and I finally fell into an uneasy sleep.

*

Looking in the local paper the following morning, I saw that Beryl Cartmell was appearing at Kingston spiritualist church that afternoon. I made up my mind to see her again as she was still one of the best mediums I had seen.

Unfortunately the paper had misprinted the starting time, so when I arrived, Beryl was in full flow to a packed hall. Slipping in quietly, I found a seat in the back row. Imagine my surprise when she immediately pointed to me and said, "I want to come to the lady at the back, who has just walked through the door."

The woman next to me prodded me with her elbow. "She means you love."

Putting up my hand in acknowledgment, I called out, "Thank you."

"You've had a difficult time of it over the past few weeks, but you've now decided to do something about it." Before I could answer, she continued, "And you should be standing here instead of me. I'm being told you must find a circle, because your energy is building day by day."

"Yes I know," I called out.

"Come and see me after I've finished," she said, before turning away and pointing to someone else.

When the session was over and everyone began filing out, I made my way to the platform to speak to her. "You've attracted spirit from the lower astral plane, and it's frightened you," she stated.

"I am scared. Another medium told me to sit on my own to develop. Everything seemed to go well at first, but now weird things are happening."

"You've every right to be fearful," she said. "You shouldn't be doing this alone. Each time you ask for a spirit to come through, your energy expands. Unless you give clairvoyance or healing, it will keep building up around you. When that happens, your aura appears as a brilliant light on the lower astral plane and you can draw all kinds of negative things to you. Some people can get away with developing by themselves, but you're so strong, you'll have to learn first how to control it."

"I've been told that I should sit in a circle, but I don't know what to do or where I should go to find a class."

Taking a slip of paper from her bag, she began to write something down. "The College of Psychic Studies in London is the best place to go," she said. "If you want to find out more about the psychic field or to develop your own ability, I strongly advise you to go there." She handed me the address. "Paul Beard is the president and you must pass an interview to get in, but my guide has told me you'll be accepted. Now, I'm off to have my cup of tea and I wish you luck my dear – not that you'll need it."

Thanking her I walked out, knowing in my heart that at long last I had been pointed in the right direction.

6

Good Advice

"You'll have to wait several weeks for an appointment, Mrs. Caulfield. Paul Beard is very busy," said the impersonal voice on the other end of the phone.

"I've waited a long time for this, so a few more weeks won't hurt me," I answered.

The secretary gave me a date for three weeks ahead before asking me for further details.

After all those years denying my psychic gift, I was now impatient to get moving. I was excited, knowing I would shortly have answers to some of my questions. Giving myself plenty of time for the journey, I made my way through Hammersmith and into London. Queensbury Place was easy to find as it was opposite the Natural History Museum. As I approached the main entrance of the old impressive house, I sensed a positive aura surrounding the building. I felt it calling to me, whispering that at last, I had found my pathway.

As I made my way to the reception area, I realised I was early. The reception area was sited within the library, so the receptionist invited me to look through the books whilst I waited. The place wasn't at all spooky. Lights were blazing and people came and went. There was a lot of laughter and chatter going on around me. After fifteen minutes, Paul Beard's secretary came for me and smiling, she shook my hand before asking me to follow her upstairs.

"There's no need to feel nervous Mrs. Caulfield, you'll find Paul very easy to talk to," she said as she knocked before opening the door to his office.

Paul came from behind his desk and greeted me warmly before gesturing to another chair. "Make yourself comfortable and then you can tell me why you're here."

As I began to speak, a floodgate opened and a torrent of words and emotion poured out. Paul listened without interruption until I concluded with what I had been told by Beryl Cartmell.

"There's no doubt you're mediumistic, because I can see that for myself but it's important that you learn how to control it. If you don't, it will control you and prevent you from leading any kind of normal life."

"My life is already far from normal. More than anything else, I need to find out how to cope with this and to understand it."

Looking at me thoughtfully, he said, "I would like you to join us here as a student, but I'm trying to decide which class would be suitable for you. I'll take you to meet Elizabeth Farrell, one of our teaching mediums and we'll go on from there."

As I followed Paul downstairs, I knew I had overcome the first big hurdle to psychic enlightenment. Beryl's guide was right. I had just been invited to join the College.

We stopped outside a closed door. Paul put his ear against it and listened for a moment before knocking. It was opened by a middle-aged lady with grey hair and spectacles. When introduced to her, I had the impression of a quiet and gentle woman. Paul briefly explained to Elizabeth about my interview and asked if she had the time to see me. She glanced at her watch. "I can spare a few minutes now, before my circle," she answered.

I had mixed emotions as I shook Paul's hand. I thanked him for his invitation to join the College.

"You won't be a student for long," were his parting words as he left the room.

Elizabeth asked me to sit facing her. After looking at me for a moment or two, she closed her eyes. When she opened them again, she shook her head from side to side. My heart sank. She didn't want me. "I'm told you're not suitable for my circle."

Seeing my look of disappointment she reached out and touched my hand. "Don't worry dear. It's because you are too strong for me. There is a need to instill discipline and control. I'll have a word with my colleague, Ivy Northage. There may be a place for you in her class." Asking me to stay where I was, she left the room. Within minutes she was back bringing Ivy with her.

Ivy's aura was different to Elizabeth's. Still kind and positive, but with a palpable inner strength that leaped out and touched me. She was a lady with a sense of discipline that people did not mess around with. I was already in awe of her. She looked at me, and without any hesitation said, "Yes. I'll definitely have you. You're just what we need. I'll tell the desk to put you on my list for my new class and we'll be in touch." With that, she said goodbye and walked out of the room.

After thanking Elizabeth, I left the college feeling elated, although I did not have a clue as to what was waiting ahead of me.

7

I Go to College

"In a few moments we will turn off the main lights, leaving only this red bulb," said Ivy. "One or two of you may turn out to be physical mediums, so it's important that no bright light or natural light should penetrate this room."

Standing up and walking to the centre of the circle, she continued, "If any of you see someone who appears to be unconscious or asleep, you're not to speak loudly or touch them. They may have spirit trying to build up in the ectoplasm from the circle and any loud noise or sudden movement can be dangerous for the medium. The ectoplasm will shoot back into their body causing them pain and physical damage. As we go along you will learn about the different types of mediumship, but for now I want to see what you're made of."

Retreating to her chair she turned to a lady sitting next to her. "This is Janet, my assistant. She will open the class in prayer and then tell you what to do. Whilst she is doing this, I will be tuning into each of you to see where your abilities lie. So, Janet, can you turn off the lights please?"

The room was plunged into darkness except for the soft glow of red, and once my eyes adjusted I found I could see reasonably clearly. Janet began to speak. "It's important to be comfortable, so loosen any tight clothing, take a few deep breaths and thoroughly relax yourselves. I'll then open in prayer."

For a few moments there came the noise of shuffling feet and deep sighs, before all became quiet again. Janet softly asked for God and our guides and friends in spirit to draw close with love and protection before turning once again to us.

"There are seven major psychic centres, or chakras, in the body. These lie near important nerve endings and close to the endocrine glands. It's these seven that must be developed for mediumship, and they in turn activate the many smaller centres surrounding them." She continued. "Each centre has its own function in psychic work, and the first one can be found at the base of the spine. This chakra provides the energy required for the other centres to work proficiently."

Ivy closed her eyes and she appeared to be asleep.

"The second centre is the largest and is in the area of the solar plexus. It's known as the centre of negativity and anything uncomfortable is felt here. It's used in all forms of mediumship, but especially for physical phenomena. It is extremely sensitive to any influence but only through feeling. It must work in conjunction with the others to have a clear understanding of spirit."

This explained why my stomach always churned so much whenever I had a premonition that something awful was going to happen.

"The third centre lies in the region of the spleen. This works together with the second centre but on a slightly faster vibration. It filters out the good feelings from the bad and it is also used for astral travel. The fourth is situated in the region of the heart and is used with the others for healing. It is here that we feel compassion and understanding. The pain and anxiety of the patient can be felt by the healer. It's also the doorway between these emotional chakras and the faster, mental chakras that follow."

Listening to this was fascinating. To have what appeared to be a logical explanation for the way everything worked made it all seem so normal.

"Centre number five is found in the area of the throat and is used for clairaudience. This is where you will hear spirit speaking and it works with the spleen and heart centres for trance mediumship. The best-known centre is number six. It's the clairvoyant eye, and is found between the eyebrows, so it is often referred to as the third eye. It's the seat of genuine clairvoyance, and once this has been experienced, it can never be mistaken for imagination. It has a dimensional quality, allowing you to see all around it, whereas a subconscious image is flat, and more like a television picture. Centres five and six work together, but one of them will be more dominant. Finally, we have centre number seven. This is known as the crown chakra and its function is purely spiritual. It is through here that spirit draws close, only operating on truth and sincerity. As energy is drawn up through the slower centres to the crown, it awakens a spiritual or cosmic consciousness. It's also through here that we cleanse all the other centres after use."

Taking a deep breath, she looked around the circle at our faces. She then turned to Ivy who now had her eyes open. Without saying anything, Ivy nodded to her.

Turning back to the circle Janet said, "We're now going to try and activate these chakras. Close your eyes, making sure you are still comfortable and relaxed. Take your mind to the base of your spine and try to visualise a glass tube going through your body and out through the top of your head." She paused for a moment before continuing. "Now, begin to see the base of this tube filling up with light. With your mind, draw this light through from centre number one to centre two." Again she paused and then said, "Right – you seem to have managed that well. Now, swing out with your mind as though you are writing a capital letter D, and go back to the base of the spine. Pull this light up again through centre two and up to three."

She continued like this through the other centres. I found that my "glass tube" kept filling up before I concentrated on it, but I still went over it again. By the time the light was going out through the top of my head, I had a job to see the base of the tube. I felt as though I had grown several feet in height and I had an ache in my throat and a pain in my forehead.

Janet and Ivy were talking quietly, so, awaiting the next instruction, I opened my eyes. Opposite me, a young woman was lying slumped in her chair. She was leaning to one side, looking as if she was about to fall. It was her they were talking about and Ivy again warned us not to touch her. Janet turned to the class and said, "You've all opened up your centres ready for work. Now go back to the base of that glass tube and simply bring the light straight through and out of the top of the head. Do this several times."

I felt as if a part of me was floating and then the lilac mist began to form. Soon, the old familiar feeling of paralysis began creeping over me. Making a huge effort, I made myself move and opened my eyes. The woman opposite was still slumped in her chair, and everyone else was still and quiet.

"Sue," asked Ivy, "tell me how you felt when you did that exercise?"

Sue licked her lips and answered slowly. "It felt as though the top of my head was going to blow away. I had a strong pain in my forehead as well."

Ivy said, "When you first activate your chakras you will get different sensations throughout your body. The feeling in your head shows you've succeeded in bringing your energy right up and out through the crown centre. The pain across your forehead indicates that you've successfully opened your clairvoyant eye. You've made a good start." Turning to me she said, "Ann, there is a man in spirit standing beside you. Can you describe him to me?"

Taken by surprise, I glanced out of the corner of my eye. "I can't see anyone, "I answered, half-expecting to see a solid figure.

"Yes you can," she said crisply. "Close your eyes again and bring your energy up once more to the third eye and then gently look with your mind." She paused for a moment. "That's right. Now tell me what you can see?"

Following her instructions, a vision of a man appeared in my mind. He was laughing and I felt that it was at my expense. "He's wearing a brown jacket and trousers, with a trilby style hat tipped back on his head."

"That's right, now describe his features and build."

Concentrating on his face, his image became so vivid that he could have been standing in front of me. "He has a pale complexion and light blue eyes. His hair is brown and straight and has receded a little. His build is slim, and he's about five foot ten inches in height."

"Now take up energy to your throat and repeat to me what he's telling you."

My throat ached and I wanted to stretch my neck. I could see his lips moving, but I couldn't hear anything. I brought the energy through again. Once more I listened as I saw his lips move, but I still couldn't hear anything.

"You're straining to hear now," Ivy said. "Relax. That's better. Now tell me what you think he's trying to say."

No matter how hard I tried, I couldn't hear him.

"Just tell me, off the top of your head, what you want to say. Forget about yourself and say anything, even if it sounds stupid to you."

"He said he died of lung cancer after a long illness," I replied quickly.

"Exactly," said Ivy. "Now tell me where that came from?"

"It just popped into my head," I said.

"That's because he put it there. Now tell me where in your head it seemed to come from?"

Thinking for a moment, I said, "Well, it seemed to come from the right side near my ear, and then it was everywhere. But it all happened so quickly."

"That's because the mental chakras work on a very fast vibration. As soon as you hear it, you should repeat it, because the next part will immediately follow."

Looking at me intently she said, "He's just told you something else, hasn't he? Before I could answer, she went on. "He died several years ago and this is the first chance he's had to make contact with anyone. Is that right?"

Amazed that she could hear him too, I nodded my head and said, "I felt that's what I wanted to say."

"Your clairvoyance is good but your clairaudience is dominant. In other words, you hear more clearly than you see, although both of them mostly work together. It's better to have them working that way round, because you do not need to see a picture to hear spirit, but you do need to hear to understand why you're being shown something."

By this time she was pacing up and down the middle of the circle. "No doubt your throat aches doesn't it?" she said with a smile.

"Yes it does – and my forehead."

"Well, that will wear off. It's because you're not used to stimulating those muscles. Once you get used to opening up, you won't feel pain any more. But right now, it's a good sign because it shows you've opened your chakras properly." Sitting down, she turned away and asked a young man what he was feeling. The girl opposite was still slumped in the same position. There were several others who were similar to me, and I found it interesting that Ivy could also see and hear everything that they could. Just before the end of class the slumped girl began to come round. She sat up with a puzzled look, and Ivy explained that she had been unconscious throughout the class. The girl said that she didn't remember a thing after taking the energy up to the heart centre.

"You definitely have trance potential," Ivy explained. "You will learn to recognise the signs of spirit trying to work through you in that way. This is one of the reasons why it's so important to work in a circle with others. You must not practice at home on your own until you've developed more, as it can be dangerous. Now Janet will close you down, and the closing procedure is something you can practice at any time. It's very easy for your centres to open. You only have to think of anything psychic and they automatically begin to fill with energy."

Nodding to Janet she once again sat down and closed her eyes.

"The crown chakra and the base chakra always stay open," began Janet. "This is because the physical energy needed each day is contained at the base of the spine. The crown chakra stays open to allow you to cleanse your other centres after closing. Therefore, we begin to close with the clairvoyant eye. With your mind, visualise the light in the glass tube receding. Once it has reached the throat, try to see a door closing in the region of the third eye. When you have done this, do the same again with your throat chakra. Continue through the other chakras until the light recedes to the base of your spine. The solar plexus is the largest centre and the most difficult to close, so pay particular attention to this area."

It wasn't as easy to close the centres as it was to open them. By the time I had reached my solar plexus I had to go over the procedure several times, as my "door" seemed to keep opening again.

"Once you've managed this, go back to the crown centre and visualise a white light flooding through your body. Bring it through your chakras, your arms and legs and out through your feet. This light is washing your centres clean from everything you've done in class. It will leave you feeling fresh and "grounded" again." She added, "Are you aware of how much warmer this room is now?"

That was true. I had found myself feeling very cold during the class but the temperature had noticeably risen as we closed down.

Janet finished in prayer, thanking God and spirit for drawing close to help us.

After the class had ended, students rushed over to them both asking questions, but Ivy told them only to remember what we had done in class and to keep closing down. There would be plenty of time for questions it seemed, once our development began in earnest.

The lady sitting next to me asked me what I thought about the class.

"I found it fascinating," I told her, "and I'm already looking forward to next week."

"It was a bit too serious for my liking," she said, "it was like being back at school. I don't think I'll be staying long if this is the way it's going to be."

"You have to give it a chance. It'll probably lighten up once we've been coming a while," I answered.

As we said goodnight, I was wishing that we were coming back the following evening instead of having to wait a week. I was euphoric. I loved it. And I liked Ivy. There wasn't anything airy-fairy about her. Her no-nonsense approach appealed to me. At last, I knew I had found what I had been searching for.

8
My First Controlled Experiences

Even after marrying Pete, there still had been times when I would lie awake at night in tears. Our relationship was strong, but that old sensation of something missing from my life had often left me feeling empty and lonely. My classes changed that forever. Being with people like me helped me and brought me a sense of peace. Embracing spirit made me see that I had been searching for something that I already had. By not wanting to be different, I had denied myself the use of a wonderful and unique gift. As the weeks went by, I was surrounded with love from my spirit friends. They drew close to me of their own accord, helping and encouraging me along a rocky pathway. The development wasn't easy. Learning to differentiate between a thought and a spirit voice took a lot of practice. Bringing up energy, recognising spirits, looking and listening to them and giving a message to someone at the same time, was difficult.

There were several students who gave up and left the class, including my friend who thought it was too serious. It was serious – but it had to be! To put it bluntly, we were being contacted by people who had died. This was something incredible, and not something that could be joked about. Ivy was strict. If you hadn't opened your chakras properly, she knew, and would make you go over everything again and again until you got it right. She worked as hard, if not harder than everyone else, and her discipline was just what I needed. Now that my energy was being released and used in a positive and controlled way, I developed very quickly. There were many students like me, but there were also others who had the ability to develop psychically, but not to a mediumistic level. These people could still develop their psychic awareness and put it to good use if they wanted to, and learning to do this would enable them to know themselves on a much deeper level.

Thousands of years ago our psychic senses were highly evolved in hunting for food and scenting danger. Now these senses have been mostly submerged by technology and therefore, not used to their full potential. Developing our intuition will help us to lead a more harmonious life.

As The College of Psychic Studies was interested in all types of psychic phenomena, there were many people who developed along different pathways to me. If we wished, we could make appointments to have readings with other mediums or to see the many varied types of mediumship demonstrated. Usually the demonstrations had to be booked weeks in advance, especially if they were unusual - such as transfiguration. This is known as physical mediumship, in which spirit uses a coarser type of energy known as ectoplasm in order to mould its own features over the mediums face. It has become quite rare, mainly because of the dangers to the medium, and because mental mediumship (a much faster vibration) has taken over.

When Spiritualism was new, physical mediumship was the only form used to prove to people that life still existed when the physical body died. Mediums would sit in a darkened room with only the glow of a red lamp. After putting themselves into a deep trance, a thick, white ectoplasm would exude from an orifice in the body. This dense energy was moulded into the form of the spirit coming through. Once spirits had clothed themselves in this way, they could walk around the onlookers, where they could be touched. They often felt quite solid, but sometimes if the ectoplasm was thinner, they were only half formed. Nearly all physical mediums suffered from bad health, because so much energy was needed for their task that they would usually be exhausted afterwards. Any kind of shock to the system (a light or loud noise) would cause the ectoplasm to contract, taking any dust or dirt into the physical body along with it.

Other demonstrations included trance, where spirit spoke through the medium, automatic writing where the mediums hand was taken over to write messages, and psychic art, where the medium would draw the spirits they could see. Needless to say, I was amazed at what I encountered, and there were a few different avenues I would eventually try for myself.

On a personal level, I discovered more about my own mediumship. I had experienced OBEs almost from babyhood, but it was not until I reached adolescence that my psychic energy became more prevalent. As the psychic centres interact with important nerve endings, hormones appear to play a large part in the development of psychic ability. Because of this, the mediumistic youngster has to contend with sensitivities well above the norm. Most mediums will tell you they had a lonely childhood and that they felt as though they were set apart from others. Like me, they thought they wouldn't be understood by their family or friends, so they suppressed what was happening to them. Now, most people are aware there is more to life than the physical aspects that we see every day. Minds are opened and questions are being asked, and people are searching for the meaning of life. Mediums are normal people who have an unusual ability. They are no different from anyone who is gifted in music, art or anything else. They only differ between themselves as to the direction their mediumship takes them. With me, my direction was rather unusual.

9

An Explanation for my Nightmares

Watching and waiting, I stand in the shadows of this desolate wasteland. Only dust and blackened stumps of trees scatter the surface. A warm wind is blowing tumbling purple clouds over the darkening landscape. I seem to be alone, but although I cannot see the others I am aware of their presence. A ripping sound reverberates through my senses. My pulse quickens as the earth opens in front of me, the noise escalating to a screaming pitch as it widens. An oily liquid ripples the abyss with a harsh mutter of sound. I look away and watch as a soft glow radiates across the barren desert. Becoming brighter, its brilliance pierces the bleak horizon, spreading until its reflection skims the crest of the chasm. Turning back again, I see an arm silently break through the surface, the hand stretching towards the radiance. An intensity of hope and longing pervades this void. And another "lost" soul is saved.

*

For as long as I can remember, this dream used to come to me once or twice a month. Although I wasn't frightened by it, I found the dream disturbing, especially as I had it so often. On some level I realised it meant something important, but no matter how I tried to rationalise what I saw, I still couldn't make sense of it. Eventually, I was woken by the dream and it wasn't long before my sleep was disturbed, leaving me tired and irritable the following day. Then I began to have another dream, which, although different in its manifestation, still had a similar ending. Not only that, but it was shown to me several times in my meditations.

*

I am flying at great speed through outer space, until above me a golden radiance appears and draws me towards a planet. I find myself slowing, before rising through swirling violet and lilac mist. My feet touch the surface of this world, which is so familiar to me. I have been here many times since being born into my physical domain. It is my spiritual home and as real to me as anything in my present life. Oron, my spirit friend takes my hand and leads me into the Temple of Life and Death. Already there are three helpers waiting, clothed in their robes of protection. They come to me and place a cloak of midnight blue around my shoulders, lifting the hood to shield my face. We wait. In front of us, the floor of the Temple begins to split until it's a wide and jagged pit filled with blackness. Holding hands we walk towards it, and distant sounds of screeching and laughter rise to greet us. Stepping from the edge, we slowly descend into the murky depths. There are wide, jagged ledges in this pit, and on each is a "lost" soul. Paedophiles, murderers and the depths of humanity reside here, on the lower astral plane. Some reach out to us as we go about our work. When they do, I touch each one gently and the helpers carry him upwards towards the light.

*

On one of my visits to Muriel Miller, my Spanish guide told me that during sleep, I did rescue work on the astral plane. I asked her what she meant by this.

"After death, you're not transformed into an angel. Your personality is still the same as when you were alive. The astral plane is the nearest to our earth and most people return to this level. More evolved spirits return to the plane above which is reserved for those who are chosen to do special work for humanity. Then there is the lower astral plane. This is the level that draws those people who have committed evil acts."

"So there is a Hell then?"

"No. Heaven and Hell do not exist as portrayed in the Bible. Spirits on the lower level have every opportunity to progress towards the light. When you are in spirit, you no longer have a physical body, so communication is by thought. Those residing on the lower level think they are still in the same situation as on the earth. Therefore, you and the others have to make them realise that what they are doing isn't actually happening. You have to change their thought processes. Furthermore, they have to want to do this. It's the same as on the earth, child. Most people tend to mix with their own kind, and after you die your spirit still does this. When you leave the earth, you only shed your old physical overcoat to wear something lighter. Apart from that, you are still the same person.

"But how does this involve me?" I asked.

"It needs a certain type of spirit to do rescue work. You need to be strong and not easily frightened by what you encounter. There are others like you and you mostly work together. Think about it, child; you wouldn't put yourself in a dangerous situation on earth without protection, so neither would you whilst you're working on the astral plane."

"What exactly is it that I do?" I asked.

My guide continued, "Whilst your body sleeps your spirit travels to the astral plane. You are then taken with others to the lower level to see if anyone is ready to progress towards a better existence. You are one of many who help to bring them into the light. It's a little like entering the prison system to rehabilitate some of the worst criminals."

"Would the nightmares I've been having, be connected with this?"

"Describe them to me, child?" she asked.

"Everything is dark and I'm descending through the centre of a huge black pit. There are grotesque people lying on ledges, who reach out to touch me. Some of them are naked and surrounded by the bones of human beings, whilst others are counting piles of money."

"Yes. I feel you are right. But what you see is mainly symbolic," said my guide.

"Symbolic or not, they're pretty awful." I answered.

"If you don't wish to remember the dreams, we can take the memory away from you."

"I'm more than willing to do the work, but would be grateful not to remember it."

So they did. From that night onwards, I no longer had what I believed were nightmares. However, I was told by spirit that my rescue work continued in my sleep and while I meditated.

Some time later, when I had been working as a professional medium for three years, I was woken by Nicky calling out in her sleep. I went to calm her, and she told me she had had a nightmare about a black pit, with grotesque people reaching out to touch her. My stomach turned over. I realised that she too was rescuing lost souls. When I returned to bed, I asked my guides to take the memory away from her. As far as I am aware, she never had the nightmare again.

10

Peter becomes a Healer

I had only been in the class for a short time, when Pete became ill. He was eating well, but he had begun to lose weight. Although it was winter, he was so hot that he lay tossing and turning on top of the bedclothes at night. Refusing to go to the doctor in the hope it would sort itself out, it got to the stage where he was shaking so badly he could not sleep. Finally he admitted he needed help.

Realising that he was very ill, our doctor sent him to hospital the same day and he was diagnosed with an over-active thyroid gland. His condition was serious and he was prescribed thirty tablets a day, plus a regular appointment to check his progress. After a few weeks the consultant told him he had the choice of taking tablets for the rest of his life, an operation on his thyroid gland, or radiotherapy. Not surprisingly, he chose to have the tablets. Although offered to him, it was then pointed out that the tablets were expensive and would become a drain on the health service. Some choice! No way did Pete want either of the other two options, so he stuck with the tablets.

"You could try spiritual healing," I suggested. "Kingston church hold regular healing sessions, and you've nothing to lose by trying."

So one evening we attended a service and inquired about the healing sessions. Choosing to sit in the front row, we found ourselves right next to the organ. Just before the service started, a huge man dressed in a coat with a heavy sweater beneath it and wearing a scarf around his neck, slowly walked over to the organ and sat down on the stool ready to play. It was far from cold in the church, and I fully expected him to remove some of his clothing, but he didn't. He took his time sorting out the music, and every now and again he would slowly turn his head to smile at us. As he began to play, I became very aware of Pete shuffling his feet, shaking and wiping perspiration from his twitching face. The contrast between them both was striking, and I couldn't help grinning. After the service, the organist struck up a conversation with us, and we discovered that he had an under-active thyroid, causing him to have the opposite symptoms to Pete. Just before leaving, Pete arranged to come the following week to see a healer by the name of Bill.

After his first session I asked him what the healing felt like.

"I sat in a chair with my back to him and the healer put his hands on my head and said a short prayer. After leaving his hands on my head for a while longer, he then moved them slowly down my spine. I felt a lot of heat and within a few minutes I had stopped shaking."

Amazed by this, I asked, "is that all he did?"

"It's difficult to believe but it's true. It lasted about fifteen minutes and I felt totally relaxed afterwards. Bill was easy to talk to and he suggested having six sessions to see how I get on."

Each time he went for healing there was an improvement, and the hospital consultant was surprised to find Pete responding so well, so he began to reduce his tablets. After six weeks, Pete was feeling much better but he was not cured, so he continued with healing. Three months later he was taken off medication completely, as tests showed his thyroid was working normally again. We both knew it was the healing that had cured his condition, as the tablets were only a means of keeping it under control. Feeling the consultant would be sceptical, Pete didn't tell him what he had been doing. As far as we were concerned though, the cure was a small miracle.

Each time he went to the church, Pete would stay behind afterwards and chat to Bill about the healing. He found himself becoming more and more interested in developing as a healer himself. Since the age of twenty-five, the joints along my spine had been degenerating and at times were very painful, so I asked Pete to try healing on me. At first he refused, saying he was not good enough and that it would not work, but despite his excuses he was eventually persuaded. We had set aside a small room in our house where we could sit quietly to meditate or give absent healing. As this room was used solely for this purpose, the atmosphere was spiritual and peaceful.

"I'll sit quietly for a few minutes and call you when I'm ready," he said.

After sitting sideways on the chair to make it easier for him to touch my back, he placed his hands on my head, before asking spirit healers to come through to use him as a healing channel. No sooner had he done this than I could feel warmth on my head. After a few moments, he moved his hands down my back coming to a halt in the lumbar region. Heat flooded the lower part of my back, getting hotter as he moved his right hand across to my hip. This was the area where pain sometimes radiated along the sciatic nerve and down my leg. Keeping his right hand in this position, he then placed his left hand in the centre of my back. The heat intensified, followed by the sensation of fingers probing along my spine. This, coupled with the heat, made me feel queasy. I was about to ask him to stop, when he lifted his hands back to my head. He then closed down, thanking his healing guides for coming through and working with him. After he had finished, the queasiness disappeared and I was so relaxed that I did not want to get up from the chair. When

I opened my eyes I found it hard to believe that the healing had taken only a few minutes.

"How do you feel?" asked Pete.

"Great; but I was beginning to feel yucky towards the end. I think it was a combination of the heat and you kneading my spine."

"It wasn't me kneading your back," he replied, "I didn't move my fingers. Neither did I feel my hands get hot. But I had the sensation that someone was lifting my hands and placing them in the right position."

"There's no doubt in my mind that you're a healer, love; the energy was so strong. It looks as though you were guided to that church to find out about it."

Within the hour the pain eased and the following day my back felt better, although a little tender in places.

Each week Pete gave me healing and the sensations varied. The heat was always there, but at times I felt as though fingers were moving along my spine and at other times as though I had pins and needles. It certainly seemed to keep my back more flexible and to keep the pain at bay, but it did not cure the problem. This didn't worry me. I knew that once something was worn, it could not be renewed. I was thankful the healing was helping the pain and, hopefully, slowing down the degeneration. I also realised that it was important for me to help myself as well. There was no point in spirit giving me healing, if I continued to do the gardening or lifting heavy weights.

Pete gave me healing on a regular basis, so his confidence grew. It was not necessary for me to tell him where the problem lay, as his hands invariably found the troubled area for themselves. He knew it was spirit giving the healing, but nevertheless, was proud that they considered him a worthy vessel.

"If we can help to alleviate pain in some small way, you on an emotional level, and me on a physical level, then I for one will know I've accomplished something worthwhile in my life," he told me.

As my healing progressed, I became aware of the spirit guides who worked with Pete. Afterwards, I would describe them, and although he could not see them for himself, he began to differentiate between them through his feelings.

If he had his Arab guide (a huge man with a great sense of humour), he would feel as though his body was stretching in all directions. If it was his little doctor guide, he would lean over and his movements became slower and more precise. These guides showed themselves to me without speaking, because the energy was being concentrated into the healing. Nevertheless, his Arab guide did tell me one day that Pete should begin working with other people. Although feeling nervous about taking this further, he agreed to start with people he knew before taking on strangers. It was while we were discussing this, that I remembered how Kishore had told me several years previously that Pete would join me in my work. Pete had been adamant that he would not become involved in the psychic field, but he had also gradually found himself drawn along the path that destiny had mapped out for both of us.

*

Each week, Ivy would impress upon us that we must stop feeling self-conscious when working. We needed to forget about ourselves, put our egos to one side and allow spirit to draw near. It was only natural for us to question what we were seeing or hearing, but she would make us go over our messages until we got them right.

"You do not say, "I think" or "I feel" when giving information. You say "I am being told to tell you" or "I am being shown". You're the telephone line transmitting the message and you must be positive in your delivery."

Slowly, I learnt to control the energy. There was no need to visualise the white light in a tube, for I found it faster and easier to use my mind. The pain in my forehead quickly disappeared, as did the ache in my throat. Each week Ivy would teach us about the psychic mechanism and the way it worked. One day she told us how the aura had been discovered.

A Dr. W. J. Kilner of St. Thomas' Hospital, London, found that the first layer of the aura could be seen and photographed. His evidence showed the aura to be a field of energy that is constantly moving, and that the inner edge can be seen with the physical eye. This inner band is called the etheric body, and it surrounds two further bands that intermingle with each other. The second band appears as smoke pouring from the body or it resembles the shimmer of a heat-haze. The last band is full of colour, with lights and shapes darting towards and away from the physical body. These last two bands can only be seen by the clairvoyant. There are some mediums who can "read" the colours, lights and shapes in the aura, but this is rare. Although I often see this level of the aura, I certainly can't read it, and I only know of one person who can.

Guardian angels, doorkeepers and guides were also explained. Guardian angels are spirit companions who surround all of us throughout our lives. The doorkeeper is the intermediary between the guardians and the guides who work with the medium. The guides are responsible for any mediumship, in addition to the well-being of the medium.

The coloured lights that I first saw in childhood were explained as "spirit lights". Spirits do not have physical bodies, so this is how they appear in their pure form. For a medium to give a description of someone before he died, the dead person must clothe himself in an astral body.

Healers appear as blue lights and the white, silver and gold are the spirits of friends, relatives and guides. Whenever I sit quietly, in prayer or absent healing, spirits show themselves to me in this way, where I acknowledge them and thank them for coming.

Making my way through the library one evening, I found Ivy waiting for me. "I'd like you to join my intermediate class at the SAGB, Ann. You need to be "stretched", and as I'm sure you'll make a good platform medium, you need to develop in a different direction."

My stomach flipped. "But I haven't been in this class for two minutes. I don't think I'm good enough to develop further."

"Why don't you let me be the judge of that," she answered, as she turned and walked away.

11
Spiritualism and Mediumship

The Spiritualist Association of Great Britain is located in Belgrave Square, London. The SAGB, as it is more commonly known, is in a magnificent Georgian building, complete with stone pillars outside the front door, facing a small park filled with flowers and shrubs. The building inside is huge, with many rooms leading off corridors and a lift to take you to the top floor for healing. Ivy had her own school based there, called The Ivy Northage School for Mediums and Psychic Studies, and she was recognised as the best teaching medium in the British Isles. Although the SAGB is known mainly for Spiritualism and the development of the medium, other classes are held for healing. People can come to demonstrations and lectures and they can make appointments for private readings. There is an extensive library that contains many items of interest, such as the tiny imprints in clay made by spirit children during the time when physical mediumship was in demand. In the waiting room, there is a bust of Abraham Lincoln, who was an ardent spiritualist, in addition to photographs of mediums taken with spirit forming in their ectoplasm. Like the College, the SAGB is a very busy place, with people making appointments for various classes, readings or healing, and there is a lot of chatter and laughter to be heard.

Making my way upstairs for my first afternoon class, I realised that only a few months before I had been desperately searching for direction, and now I was well on my way to working as a medium. For years I had walked a reluctant path, and yet over the past few weeks I had undergone a complete reversal. Without any doubt, this was my destiny, and I had never been happier or felt more at peace.

Walking into the room where Ivy held her intermediate class, there was a bounce in my step and a smile on my face. I was early, so I pulled out a chair and sat quietly with closed eyes in the rays of the sun streaming through the windows. Feeling spirit drawing close, I gave thanks for their patience and guidance over the years.

*

"Jane. Forget about yourself and everyone here. The message will flow once you get rid of the "I" factor. Every time you give a message, you say, "I think" or "I feel". Be more confident. You know there is someone with you. You know what they are telling you. So don't say, "I think" or "I feel" again!"

Jane flushed a delicate shade of pink and apologised. Turning back towards Sarah, she drew a deep breath and began to speak. "Standing behind you is a man who was about sixty-five or seventy years of age when he passed over. He has very light grey, receding hair and a small, grey moustache. He gives the impression of being about five feet eight inches tall, with a small build." She paused. "He is dressed in a black suit with a matching waistcoat. Threaded through the waistcoat is a gold watch-chain. He's wearing a small, black hat, and holding a large, leather bag." Pausing again, she took another deep breath. "I think he's a doctor."

"Right, you can stop there, Jane. That was much better. Do you see how positive you were in your description and delivery? You let it down at the end though. If you know what you can see, say 'He is a doctor', not 'I think.'"

Jane quickly returned to her seat and Ivy called someone else out to give a reading.

This class was totally different from the one at the College. There was no red light as everything was done in daylight with the curtains open. Ivy made us take it in turns to walk around the circle, while "tuning" into spirit. It was a far quicker process, and it was much harder to do. I found that I could give a good, clear reading with one person, but then really struggled with someone else. We were taught that, although our mediumship could be similar to that of others, our own was unique, and it was necessary to develop and fine-tune our own abilities rather than emulate someone else's.

"As you develop you'll find yourselves becoming far more sensitive to noise," she explained. "This in turn will make you irritable. When this happens, find somewhere quiet to sit. Bring the white light through the whole of your body, and after a few minutes you'll find yourself feeling calmer."

This was something I had been aware of for years, but in the short time I had been in the classes, I had noticed how much my sensitivity had heightened. I couldn't tolerate the noise of motorbikes, or anything similar. Any sudden, loud noises would cause a white, hot flash of pain in my solar plexus. And I hated shopping. If I felt happy and energetic before walking into a store, I was a miserable, wet rag by the time I came out. We were told this was due to picking up fleeting emotions from all the people we passed or were in contact with. Bringing the white light through my body definitely helped. When I did this my fingers and toes tingled, proving that mental application could produce physical sensation.

Gradually, we took Ivy's discipline on board, and by this time I had begun to practice at home. There was no shortage of volunteers, for most people found the subject fascinating and loved to sit for me, even if I was a bit slow and stilted at times. Of all the other pathways we were told about and shown, the one that fascinated me the most was psychometry. Psychometry is the art of reading the aura of an article. This can be anything from a stone, a piece of wood, crystal or jewellery. An aura surrounds every single thing and through this method we can tell the past and present, but not the future. With a stone, a good psychometrist can see a volcanic eruption and feel its heat. Alternatively, they may experience the coldness of the sea and have visions of the depths of the ocean. A piece of wood can show the birth or death of the tree that it came from and a crystal can show how it was formed.

In some Spiritualist churches, psychometry is allowed, although it is not classed as mediumship.

People brought in pieces of jewellery, keys or other items that belonged to them or that had belonged to people who had died. The medium would pick an item from the tray, hold it up and describe it. Then she would hold it between her fingers whilst rubbing it gently, at the same time expressing her thoughts on what she was feeling or seeing. Once finished, she would do the same with each of the other items. This form of vibration is very fast, and again it's important to say whatever is seen or felt, no matter how daft it may appear to be. What doesn't make sense to the medium could well make sense to the owner of the article.

Ivy showed us how to do this, but she would not allow it during a lesson. She explained that if a medium was struggling with a reading, it sometimes helped to hold an item of jewellery from a deceased person. This would often lead to clairvoyance with the deceased spirit making contact. She emphasised that it was to be used only as a last resort or the medium would begin to rely on it. This is when mistakes can be made, and when mediums fall under the impression that spirit is conversing with them when in fact it is not.

Even when not using psychometry, Ivy was suspicious of messages that were passed on in the form of symbols, and if we received this form of message, she would insist that we went back and asked spirit for a clear picture. She said, "If spirit can show you a symbol, then they can show you the correct picture. It is laziness on the part of spirit, and if you accept this rather than demanding clairvoyance, you will not become good mediums. You must always aim for the best that can be achieved." She would reiterate the importance of this saying that, over the years mediums have been persecuted for their beliefs, poor mediumship or fraud, so it was down to us to make sure we were not ridiculed in the same way.

As an example, Ivy told us about Helen Duncan, one of Britain's best-known physical mediums, who in 1944, was the last person to be convicted under the Witchcraft Act of 1735. Police broke in and arrested her while she was in the midst of holding a séance. She was tried at the Old Bailey for fraud and imprisoned for nine months, despite many witnesses testifying to her credibility. On her release she continued with her mediumship until her death in 1956. During this time, she suffered constant bouts of ill health, which were blamed on her incarceration. Subsequent evidence has suggested that wartime authorities were not really worried about fraud, but thought she was revealing military secrets. At one of her séances, spirits of sailors materialised, with "HMS Barham" printed on their caps. It transpired that a German U-boat had sunk the battleship Barham, with the loss of many lives. News of this disaster had been kept secret by the government.

It was during this period of our development that Ivy was approached by television producers who wanted to make a program about psychics and mediums. They asked if they could film her class while the students worked. She asked us if we were happy to be in the program, but said that she would understand if we didn't want to be. At that time, interest in psychic phenomena was fairly strong, but if a television program was made on the subject, it usually was not taken seriously. Mediums would be asked to demonstrate in unsuitable conditions, such as bright lights or with loud music playing, and often with sceptical presenters poking fun at them. Despite the fact that I knew how good I knew our class could be, I personally decided against being filmed. When the program was aired, most of the filming had been edited, and what was left appeared to belittle the subject. Even now, in these enlightened times, we're still not taken seriously, for those who do appear on television are often seen as eccentric dabblers yearning for limelight, fame and fortune. Despite being asked several times to demonstrate my mediumship on one program or another, I have always refused. I prefer to stay quietly in the background, knowing that spirit will guide people to me who need help. I'm certain that if my spirit friends wanted me before a camera, despite my protests they would make sure it happened.

Before long, Ivy asked me to join her advanced class, which was held in the evening. During the day, the journey to the SAGB was reasonably easy, but I needed extra time for the rush hour journey. Leaving home at five thirty normally ensured I would be in class by seven thirty. Often I would be early, but I didn't mind waiting. Ivy would shut the door dead on seven thirty, and even if you were only a couple of minutes late, she would not let you in. She said, "If you care enough about what you're doing, you'll make the effort to get to the class on time. Rushing in at the last minute upsets the vibrations of those already here." One evening I arrived to find her involved in a shouting match with a student.

"If you don't work in the way that I teach you, then there's no point in you staying in my class."

"I am doing what you tell me, Ivy, but ..." her voice trailed off as she was interrupted.

"Don't lie to me. I was there. I saw the way you were working, and it was not mediumship. This will reflect on my teaching and I will not be responsible for your shoddy methods. I no longer want you in my class or to be associated with you."

Apparently, Ivy had watched her demonstrating somewhere, and most of what she had given as clairvoyance was rubbish. When confronted, she insisted that spirit had given her the messages, when in fact most of it was auric reading. The hapless student had completely forgotten that Ivy was more than capable of linking up with her on a spiritual level. In time I also learnt to see and hear the spirits working with my own students, and I would know if their clairvoyance was genuine.

One evening on my way to class, my car began to lose power, but I managed to steer it over to the side of the road as it came to a halt. Nothing happened when I turned the key, not even a click – it was dead. I waited before trying again, but still nothing happened. Not wanting to flood the engine, I left it a few more minutes before once more turning the key. Complete silence. Getting agitated I sat back into the seat, relaxed and brought the light through to calm me.

"Now look here spirit," I said, "I'm on my way to learn your work, and so a little help to get this car moving wouldn't go amiss. And I would be very grateful to you." I didn't expect an answer, but leaning forward, I held my breath as I turned the key again. To my relief the engine fired. Thanking my unseen friends, I pulled out onto the road and still arrived at the class before seven thirty.

12

Colour and Other Forms of Psychic Work

"Clairvoyant colours have an exquisite beauty that cannot be captured with oil paints."
Sir Winston Churchill

Win Kent is a colour therapist and clairvoyant. Not just an ordinary clairvoyant either. Her psychic work is rather special, as she is one of the rare few who can read the colours and markings of the aura. At one time, she was in the Salvation Army, but she discovered that this didn't fulfil her spiritually. Her special kind of mediumship gave her answers she couldn't find elsewhere. Win was a friend and colleague of Ivy, and she worked at the SAGB, holding classes in mediumship and the therapy and psychology of colour. To get to the SAGB, I had to travel via Hammersmith, first passing Richmond and East Sheen, where Win shared a flat with her friend Mabs. Win's classes were held at the same time as mine so it was no trouble for me to give them a lift in my car. We soon became firm friends and I found out what an exceptional person she was. My own fascination with colour led me to join her colour class.

"Colour is a living energy – pure light – and it permeates the whole of man and our world," she told us as she passed a prism around. "Prisms are used in India for healing, along with conventional medicine, because illness can often be diagnosed in this way."

We were all busily checking each other out with the prism, and calling out to Win if we found someone with different colours on her face. When we finally passed the prism back to her, she continued speaking.

"The colours are divided into magnetics and electricals, and green is the balance between the two. Red is used for the base of the spine, orange for the stomach, yellow for the area of the spleen and liver, with green at the heart centre. These are called the magnetic colours and they have a slower vibration. Blue is used for the throat area, indigo for the eyes and violet for the head; and these work on the faster, electrical vibration. An eighth ray called magenta brings them all together. Tints of all these colours can be added - and we will go into that more when we come to using the lamps and filters that we use to project the healing colours into the body. For all of you who are studying mediumship, you will find that the colour chakras lie close to the psychic centres in the body, and each colour of the spectrum correlates to its psychic partner."

Turning to a white-board, she pointed out the areas that correspond with each psychic centre. "The higher electrical colours can be used further down the body in the magnetic areas, but a magnetic colour cannot be used above its own centre. The eighth ray – magenta – is made up of infra red and ultra violet rays, which are known as the "burning" rays. However, magenta doesn't burn, even though it is classed as a magnetic colour."

She paused, looked around the class and continued. "All colours must be used in healing with their complimentary colour, and green is both the balance and complimentary colour to magenta. For this reason it can be used on the base of the spine in therapeutic healing.

"For those of you who can see the colours of the aura and who want to develop your clairvoyance this way, the following is what you should look for. The positive aspects are bright, clear colours, while the negative aspects are dull, muddy and dead looking. Dominant colours consist of habitual thought and action and these reflect the basic colours of the spectrum. Temporary colours and shapes show passing moods and emotions that are brought on by conditions or situations in that persons life." Speaking louder she said. "Specialisation is required in this field, as experience, knowledge and skill is needed to separate the two." More quietly now, she continued, "The aura expands when emotions are expressed, such as love, compassion, tenderness, music, beauty, meditation or inspiration. The colour shows the kind of emotion that is conveyed. Any form of negative emotion, such as fear, shock or drugs, will cause the aura to contract. The outline of the aura will show a distinct inward curve at any point of the physical body where there is injury or disease. The colour is then shown as a faded transparency indicating the disorder and its seriousness." As she concentrated on what she was saying, she began to speak faster, making it difficult for me to take down notes. "When a patient is being treated for referred pain, the clairvoyant can be helpful, as the problem area will be different to the one that hurts.

"Now, I want you to pair off, because you are going to try and feel the aura of your partner. A man's aura is about five to six inches in width. A woman's is wider – about eight to ten inches, although it does vary with both sexes."

While she was telling us this, everyone was busy moving chairs out of the way and soon, we were standing facing each other and waiting for the next instruction.

As a demonstration, Win stood in front of one of the women and said, "Relax yourselves and then bring your hands out to the side of your partner as far as you can." She watched us to make sure we were doing this properly. "Very slowly, move your hands in towards the body. When they meet the aura, you should feel some resistance. It may be fairly obvious, but it's more likely to be faint. Some of you will be aware of a light, tingling sensation in your fingers in addition to the resistance."

My partner tried first. She did it a little too fast and ended up without feeling anything, so she tried again. Very slowly, she brought her hands in towards me before stopping some distance away from me. Then without saying anything, she did it again, stopping in the same place as before.

"I can feel some resistance here," she said to me. "It's almost as though I want to bounce my hands off of it." She called Win over. "Can you tell me if I've got it right as I thought the resistance was further from the body than you said?"

Win slowly moved her hands in and then stopped in the same place as my partner had. "It's just here," she said. "Ann's aura has widened because we've been talking about the subject." She called out to the other students, "Most of you will find the aura wider than normal as a result of being here in the class."

When we changed over, I also found this. On touching the person's aura, a subtle tingle ran through my fingers, but it stopped when I moved through the edge of the aura. Just as I was getting the hang of it, Win called out, "Right, change over to someone else and try again."

With my new partner, I found the aura to be much closer to her body, and there was a definite resistance to my touch, almost tightness - but no tingling in my fingers. Interestingly, I had found this girl to be quite introverted, so I made up my mind to ask Win about this on the way home.

Win called out, "Sit down again, because I want to set you an experiment before you leave." "Find someone who will sit for you at home, and ask her not to wear bright clothing. Place her against a dark background with poor or dim lighting, but not in darkness. Tell her to relax, and uncross hands, legs or feet. You yourself should sit at an angle, and look diagonally at your subject to allow you to see the colours out of the corners of your eyes. These will show as small, clear flickering tongues of transparency. You should note the position against the physical body. Write down everything you see, clear or muddy colours, and how you felt about them. But, don't worry if you can't see anything, because only a few of you are clairvoyant in this way."

On the way home I asked Win if someone's aura would be affected if they were introverted.

"Yes, it can be. If that person wants to keep herself to herself and doesn't want to let anyone into her life, she could have a close aura that reflects her nature. Of course, you would have the opposite with an extrovert. Mind you, Ann, the aura is affected strongly through our emotions, and when someone is ill and in pain, it would be difficult to feel their aura at all. Many other factors could come into it. For instance, drugs can open the aura until it is very wide, and more often than not, it will stay open. This isn't a good thing, because the person can't protect herself from psychic danger or cut herself off from the negativity of other people. I'll go into all of this in my classes, so there's no point in telling you much now. You'll feel swamped, especially as you're still developing your mediumship."

"Oh Win, there's so much to learn. I really regret not coming into this earlier. I could have been working years ago if I hadn't pushed it away."

"You probably weren't meant to come into it earlier," she answered. "There were other things you had to learn along the way, and others have had to learn from your experiences. The reason you're involved in all of this isn't for yourself, but for other people. I don't mean people necessarily searching for help, but sceptics or people with closed minds in your own circle of friends or family. You're here to teach them, even though it may feel very uncomfortable at times." With that she closed the car door, gave a wave and left me thinking about what she had said.

*

"Right Ann, which colour filter would you put into a lamp if someone had sore eyes?"

"Indigo."

"And, what is the complementary colour you would use?"

"Orange."

"Good. And can you tell me how you would use the lamp on someone with this condition?"

Swallowing nervously I answered. "I would sit my patient in a comfortable position, and then put the filter in place before switching on the lamp."

"Go on."

"I would ensure that the lamp is level with the eyes and is at arms length, and tell the patient to close his eyes for two minutes. Then I would ask him to gaze directly into the indigo light."

She didn't answer, so I continued. "I would ask the patient to move his eyes to the left, and then down to the right and back to the light without moving his head."

"So far, so good," she said.

"Then I would ask him to close his eyes. I would repeat this exercise, finishing with closed eyes facing the light for a further two minutes."

"Good. And what's the maximum time for this to be used?"

"No more than five minutes for each application."

"And where would you project the complementary colour?"

"Through the solar plexus."

Giving me a smile and a nod, she turned to someone else.

Although I studied the therapeutics of colour, I had difficulty in putting my knowledge to work other than when I was in the class. I also found it impossible to buy the special lamp that was needed for use with the filters. The company was either out of stock or there would be some other problem. In the end I gave up trying. I found that I was using colour more and more on a clairvoyant level, so I told myself that this was the way I was meant to use it rather than in a practical sense. Despite this, I stayed on in the class, to study magnetic healing.

It is important to be in robust health before using magnetism on anyone, as the energy required comes from the healer and not through spirit. As with spiritual healing, the healer places her hands on the patient, but instead of asking for help from spirit, she concentrates her own energy through her hands into the patients' body. Although I was impressed with the results of magnetic healing, I found myself depleted of energy fairly quickly, so I concentrated on using spiritual methods instead. If someone found it impossible to come and see me personally, I would offer them absent healing as an alternative. For this, it was important to sit somewhere quiet, preferably in the evening or at night, when most people are either resting or asleep. I would then open up my chakras in prayer and visualise each patient in a circle of light. Concentrating my mind, I would see them happy and well. At times the light would change colour, and I would then know that spirit was intervening in the process, especially if I could see my guides with the patient. If a patient were very ill, I would try to find time to focus on them separately, picturing myself alongside my guides in order to make the energy stronger. Absent healing is very effective. Distance is no barrier where psychic energy is concerned, and it has been proved that this form of healing has had positive results on the other side of the world.

Win had so much knowledge, and I was fascinated by everything that she had to show us. She would hold candle rituals because if one is clairvoyant, one could sometimes see faces in a candle flame. At other times, there would be a light touch on the face, head or back, from spirit friends. Classes were held in music, where students learnt that each sound vibrated to a different colour. We studied crystals for their energy, and used flowers and magnetised water for healing. Flowers were used in another form of clairvoyance, known as clairsentience. This was similar to psychometry but on an even faster and higher vibration. Win also held classes for trance mediumship. I had been told several times that I would make a good trance medium, so I decided to try it.

Developing trance can be a long, drawn-out process and patience is a must. It's important that the medium in charge chooses the students carefully, making sure they are prepared to allow spirits to take over and control their body. This is known as "negative" mediumship and it means that the medium must release control to the spirits. The medium's personality must step outside of her body to allow the spirit to enter into her. The spirit must get accustomed to the physical surroundings that he finds himself in and then learn how to use them. Whilst this is happening, the medium is aware of what is going on but unable to do anything. It's a little like having an out-of-body experience. For the first two or three weeks, I sat in silence with the rest of the students waiting for something to unfold. One or two of them could be heard grunting or sighing and more than a few appeared to be asleep.

One afternoon, I was sitting with my eyes closed, when a strange feeling began to envelop me. A heavy sensation began to spread throughout my body and I thought I was going to have an OBE. As this came to mind, the sudden experience of being tipped back made me clutch the chair and cry out. On opening my eyes, I found I was still in the same position and that no one else had been disturbed by my outburst. When the class was finished, Win told me she had seen the spirit of a native, American Indian trying to step inside my body. I explained about the impression I had of falling backwards, but she said this was caused by him pushing me to one side. Because I had found it frightening, I had cried out with my mind and had thus taken control of my body again.

 After that incident, it was difficult for me to relax enough to allow spirit to come close. Eventually I gave up the class, as by now I understood that I did not want to be controlled. Maybe it stemmed from my earlier experiences, when my bed had been lifted in the air and I had seen the frightening faces. Anyway, whatever the reason, I decided to stick with "positive" mental mediumship.

Win understood the way I felt. In addition, whatever she did for anyone was always done with love. We could feel this emanating from her. Her mission in life was to heal and she could do that in so many different ways.

13

Getting it Wrong on the Platform

As part of our training, Ivy would take students to different spiritualist churches so that we could practice on the congregation. We were known as "fledglings" and the people we worked with did not expect too much from us. We all dreaded this. It was totally nerve racking and my stomach would churn like mad, despite calming measures of white light! There was one poor woman who had to stay constantly close to the restroom as she would be sick with nerves, so because of this Ivy always put her on platform last. The strange thing was though, as soon as we really got into our readings the turmoil would soon pass. By this time my clairvoyance had changed so that I could see spirit standing with the person I had to contact, and this helped to confirm what I was hearing.

One evening, Ivy arranged for us to work at a Spiritualist church in Enfield in Middlesex, just to the north of London. When we arrived I nearly died with fright. The hall was packed, and people were standing shoulder to shoulder along the walls. As students, we always sat in the front so that we could not see whom we were working with. This was necessary to make sure that members of the congregation did not draw our attention. It was important for our guides to tell us to whom we had to go, so that mistakes were not made.

I tried to calm down and push the "I" factor out of the way, but when I walked to the centre of the platform, there was a deathly silence as all eyes focused on me. "Oh God, please help me?" I asked inwardly as I looked around and saw dozens of spirit forms standing next to their loved ones. "Where do I go?" I wailed in my head.

"Do not worry, child, we are with you," came back the gentle, calm voice of my guide.

"Look to your right, just past the middle row. You will see spirit holding up her hand."

Sure enough, I could see a spirit waving to me. With a smile showing a confidence that I did not feel, I called out, "I would like to come to the lady sitting fourth from the end of the row, towards the middle. The lady in the blue raincoat."

Another woman raised her arm, even though she was not wearing anything blue.

"No, sorry not you – the lady a little further back. Yes, that's right," I called out, as the right woman raised her hand.

"There is a lady standing with you, who was about forty five to fifty years of age when she passed over. She was fairly tall and slim and always stood with a very straight back."

The lady looked puzzled as she tried to remember.

"Her hair is light brown and curly, and it reaches just below her ears. There is tightness across my chest, and she's saying she had breathing problems before she died."

Shaking her head from side to side she said, "No, I can't recall anyone like that."

"More information please?" I mentally asked my guide.

"She was ill for almost two years before she passed over," I repeated to the woman, "and she was in hospital towards the end where she had to have oxygen to help her breathing."

"No dear," the woman called back to me. "I can't accept anything you're giving me."

My face was burning and I felt such a fool, that although I was supposed to give two messages, I just could not do it.

"In that case I'll have to leave it – I'm sorry," I called back before turning and almost running from the platform.

My friend Dorothy squeezed my arm as I sat down, before stepping up to take her turn.

After we finished and we were making our way to the door, a middle-aged man approached me and asked if I could spare him a moment.

"The spirit lady you described was for me. She was my wife, and before she died, she contracted pneumonia; that's why she couldn't breathe. I was standing behind the woman in the blue raincoat."

"Why didn't you put your hand up once you realised who she was?" I asked.

"I'm really sorry, but this is my first time in a Spiritualist church, and I just felt daft knowing everyone would look at me. I wasn't expecting to get a message. She only died a month ago."

Not half as daft as I felt, I thought as I listened to him.

"Well, whatever you do, don't give up," I told him, "because I'm sure she'll come through again. It must be very difficult for you and it will take time for you to come to terms with her death. At least she isn't suffering any more."

Shaking my hand, he apologised again and then thanked me. Turning away with his head down and his slumped shoulders, he looked a figure of total dejection. Poor guy, I thought, he doesn't realise it yet, but he'll have more difficulty coming to terms with this than his wife will, but at least he had the courage to come to me, confirming the message I had given.

The problem had been my own fault, because, if I had checked with the people on either side of the woman, they might have acknowledged the message. That was another valuable lesson I learnt - people did not come to see me; they came to receive messages from spirit. I should have stopped worrying about myself and just remembered that I was only the telephone link between the spirit world and ours.

14
Practice and Graduation

"The energy used on a psychic level is the same as your physical and sexual energy," Ivy explained. "Therefore, you'll find that you cannot give readings without a break. This is very important, because if you are feeling below par then your mediumship will suffer. It is not possible to make a living from readings alone, so if you are looking for a way to earn money, you will have to find alternative avenues to work with. Mediumship is a vocation and it demands total commitment to work for the benefit of others. However, we all have to live in this world and pay our way. So just like any other specialised field of work, you should be paid for a job well done." She began to pace the floor as she concentrated on what she was saying. "By charging a fee, you have a reputation to live up to. If you don't charge and your performance is weak, you can tell yourself it doesn't matter because the sitter is not paying for it. If you have a difficult reading, you should be honest and say so. It will not benefit you to make anything up, and if you do you'll never see that person again."

This was a subject that I and other students had some difficulty with. We were aware that some mediums did not charge and that some considered that those who did so were in the wrong. Those who did not charge usually had a separate income. Many mediums lived alone without any other means of monetary support, which often meant they had to take on different types of work to supplement their income.

What Ivy said about substandard mediumship was also true, because I had often come across it in my early days while searching for the truth. While I was turning this over in my mind, Ivy had continued speaking.

"The choice is yours as I can only advise you. But whatever you do, remember that people will look to you for comfort and hope, so when they leave you, they should feel that they you have helped them."

*

We were now at the end of our training, and Ivy - strict as always - had only selected three of us for our graduation. It was summer and the ceremony was held at the SAGB in a large hall bedecked with flowers. As usual we sat in the front and were told to give two readings each before receiving our certificate. Long before the event opened, the hall was packed, and Pete and Nicky had come along to give me moral support. Although I had worked on platform as a fledgling, I knew I had to get this right because I could no longer fall back on the excuse that I was only practicing. Sitting with my other colleagues, I tried to conquer my nerves by closing myself off from everyone else in the room and concentrating solely on spirit.

"Don't worry, child, we will not let you down. Just remember your training and forget about yourself and everyone else, except for those with whom you are working." The voice was loud and clear in my head, so I relaxed a little as the first student was called up.

Ivy and Win were sitting to one side of the platform, smiling broadly to give us encouragement and willing us to do well. The first student was very nervous, but when she began her clairvoyance, she did well and I could see she was pleased once she had finished. Everyone clapped, helping to raise the vibrations. The atmosphere felt relaxed and positive, which helped me, because I was next. Up on the platform, I asked inwardly whom spirit wanted me to go to.

"Over to your left, third row, fifth lady in," came back the answer.

I scanned the audience. "Right, I've got her, thank you," I inwardly said, while I simultaneously spoke to the woman concerned.

"I'm being directed to the lady in the third row who is wearing a peach dress."

The woman put up her hand in acknowledgment.

"There is a gentleman standing with you. He was about fifty to fifty-five years of age before he died. His hair was beginning to recede, but the rest of it was still thick and dark. At one time he grew a moustache but then shaved it off. And although he wore glasses they were only for reading." Drawing breath, I went on. "He's wearing light grey trousers, a dark, checked shirt and a long-sleeved blue sweater."

"Yes. I'm sure I know who he is," she answered.

"More information please," I asked the spirit standing next to her.

"I was here one minute and gone the next," he told me.

Nodding her head she agreed, "Yes that's true."

"It was nearly two years ago, but my wife is only just beginning to come to terms with it."

After I passed on this message, she called out, "Yes, the description fits my husband, and what you say is right."

As she answered me, I drew her voice into my aura to make the energy stronger and then I became aware of a sharp pain in my chest.

"He said he passed over with a heart attack but there was no warning."

"Absolutely right," replied my lady.

"He's given me the name of David. He isn't telling me that it's his name, but that it is someone close to you."

"Yes. David is our son," she said with a smile.

"David is thinking of changing his job, but if he does, he will have to move house too."

"Yes, he will."

"Well, his dad is saying he should stop dithering and get on with it, as it's the best chance he's been given."

Then I asked, "Do you understand this message?"

The woman nodded.

"There is more information about his job, but it's private and we're unable to discuss it here."

"Yes. I understand. Thank you. I'll tell David as soon as I can."

"He's now leaning towards you and kissing your cheek. He says he loves you, but you must stop worrying about the small health problem that you have, because it's nothing."

She put one hand on her chest, and with a sharp intake of breath she nodded again. I said goodbye and turned to someone else. After mentally clearing my aura, I asked my guide whom I had to go to next.

"Over to the right, second row, second lady in." At least, that is what I thought he said.

As I came to this lady, I stated, "You have a problem with the lower part of your right leg."

"No I haven't," she said, shaking her head.

"Sorry. I've obviously got that wrong," I replied, drawing her voice towards me. My own leg and foot were hurting, so I knew I was in the right area; I asked her again, in the ridiculous hope she may have forgotten about it.

"No, I'm afraid it still isn't mine," she repeated, and I realised that the energy had now become weaker. "Am I with the young lady sitting next to you?" I asked.

"Yes, it's me, but the problem is with my foot, not my leg."

I smiled at her and said, "As your foot is on the end of your leg, its pretty close isn't it."

Luckily, most of the audience laughed, including Ivy and Win, and the energy immediately became stronger as I continued with the reading. When I finished, everyone clapped me off the platform, the third student followed and gave two successful readings. We were each presented with a certificate and a bouquet of flowers before I finally made my way over to Pete and Nicky.

"I'm glad that's over," I told them as we walked outside.

Pete gave me a kiss saying, "I thought you did well considering you had problems with the second reading.

"I know. And I shouldn't have asked a question. I just hope it gets a bit easier as time goes on."

As we approached the car, I heard someone calling my name and turning, I saw Ivy standing with a man and woman. All three were looking our way and beckoning for us to go back to them.

After introducing the others, Ivy said, "Clive and Doreen have booked several venues in Wales for psychic demonstrations and they've been looking for a good medium to go with them. I've recommended you."

They said they had been in the audience during the graduation and were impressed with the standard of mediumship from all three of us.

I asked them when they were planning on leaving.

"Next week," Clive answered. "So we need to know now if you're interested, otherwise we'll have to find someone else quickly."

"Turning to Pete, I asked, "What do you think?"

"There's no reason why you can't go. I can manage everything back home."

Facing Clive again I said, "If you're sure it's me you want then yes, I'll come."

After they left, Ivy vouched for their reputation as managers in the psychic field. We sorted out the arrangements with her, said goodbye and went on our way.

"Talk about in at the deep end," I remarked, getting into the car. "Spirit is right again. Less than a year of training and I've been booked for my first professional engagement."

15

Not All Spiritual People are Considerate

The church was full and while the chairwoman gave the prayer and address, I tuned into spirit. Clive was sitting close by because he was going to speak after I had given the clairvoyance. There had not been time to eat, as we had to rush to church for the service after several demonstrations elsewhere. My stomach decided to remind me of this, by giving out a huge growl of complaint, causing Clive to look at me with raised eyebrows. Grinning at him, I shrugged my shoulders and patted my stomach, thankful that the platform was so deep that nobody else could hear the noise. This demonstration was my last of the day and I was determined that it should go well, despite the fall in my level of energy.

"I would like to come to the gentleman in the front row sitting next to the lady in blue."

The woman nudged the man next to her and he raised his hand.

"Yes sir. If you would give a clear yes or no as we go along, I'll be able to use your voice to strengthen the energy."

"Thank you," he called out clearly.

"My guide is saying you have a problem with your eyesight."

"Yes. You could say that."

"Unfortunately, there hasn't been any improvement in this condition."

"No. There isn't any light at the end of the tunnel," he said with a smile.

"You're seeing colour though - and quite vividly."

"That's right," he answered, and the woman next to him was nodding her head in agreement.

"How can he see colour clearly if he has a problem with his eyesight?" I asked my guide.

"You'll find out in a moment," he answered.

"You're mediumistic yourself, but you work in a different way to me. This is because of the difficulty with your eyes," I said.

"That's correct. I see the colours clairvoyantly in my head. I'm blind so I work with my other psychic senses instead."

By now several of the people in the front row who knew him were laughing, knowing how close I was to his situation. It had not been possible for me to know that he could not see, for when I spoke to him he looked directly at me. From there, I proceeded with evidence from friends and family in spirit. This is another good example of giving the information exactly as it is conveyed. I would have been flummoxed had I allowed my own thoughts to interfere. The rest of the service went well, and soon enough I was able to sit down and get something to eat and to restore my energy again.

During my visit to Wales, I had expected to stay in either a guesthouse or a hotel, but I was surprised and disappointed to discover that I had to share a bedroom with a woman connected to the church. As I had not been told about this until the last minute, I had no choice but to go along with it. However, imagine how I felt when I discovered I also had to share a bed with this stranger! I was giving my services free of charge, so I could not afford to go anywhere else. It was different for Clive and Doreen. As managers, they were able to demand a fee, and had chosen to stay in a guesthouse. On our last morning I found money had been stolen from my purse, after I had left it in what should have been a safe place.

It was our last day in Wales and although Clive and Doreen knew about my stolen cash, they told me they were staying on, so I had no money and no means of getting home. I felt very let down by them and I considered that they were totally unprofessional as managers. In the end, Clive had no choice but to give me my train fare so that I could get home. Pete met me from the train, and he was disgusted when I told him what had happened. Later, we told Ivy about the whole sorry saga, and she could not apologise enough, as she had recommended these people.

Apart from that incident, the rest of my time in Wales was enjoyable. I liked the Welsh. Wherever I went they welcomed me with warmth and invited me into their homes. Later I was frequently invited to return and to give private readings alongside further platform work. As a medium I was expected to include philosophy alongside my clairvoyance, and it was these talks that often stirred up the most questions. There were many people who were concerned as to what happened to someone after they died. Most said they had been searching for answers for a long time before seeking out a medium or visiting a Spiritualist church. I tried to reassure them that death is nothing to be afraid of, and that simply put, we step from this threshold into another life. The one certainty in life is that we all die. Yet, people in this country hardly ever discuss the matter of death. Usually it is not until we begin to approach old age ourselves that we even begin to think about it. Unless of course, someone close to us dies.

Most religions believe in an afterlife of some kind. As individuals, many of us see God differently, some as a figure - others as energy and love. We may choose different pathways for our journey through life, but eventually we all return to the same source. It does not matter how we get there, only that we will. The spirit world has shown that life on the astral plane is infinitely better than on our physical one. Our earthly existence is our spiritual nursery, and we may choose to reincarnate in successive bodies, experiencing different situations to help us to spiritually progress. However, there will come a time when we no longer return to earth, and choose instead to rise higher through the spheres, reaching our ultimate destiny and becoming "At one with God."

16

The Devil Pays a Visit

Although I had graduated and I had officially become a professional medium, I was aware that this was only the beginning of my psychic journey, and that there was still much to learn. There were times when my readings did not appear to go well, and on these occasions I would apologise and end the sitting, even if my guide was insistent that the information was correct. When a sitter said "no" several times, this did not exactly fill me with confidence. I had not realised that if my reading was discussed with a third party, the information could possibly be accepted by that person, rather than the sitter. This is something that happened to me when I went along for a reading with Coral Polge, who is an international psychic artist.

Coral would touch your hands to make contact and then begin to draw the figure she was sensing in spirit. At times she would give a message as well, but mainly she concentrated on her art. When I saw her, she drew the portrait of an elderly woman. This was quite a stern looking lady, unsmiling with a no-nonsense look about her face. There was no way whatsoever that I could say I knew her, but I accepted the drawing and took it home. The picture did not ring any bells with Pete either, so I put it away and forgot about it. One day, my mother and an aunt came to see me, and although both were sceptics, we had been discussing Coral Polge, and I produced the drawing to show them. With some astonishment they agreed that the portrait was a good likeness of an aunt of theirs - someone whom I knew nothing about.

On another occasion, I was sitting quietly in my psychic room at home, when spirit showed me a funeral procession. An aunt and uncle of mine were standing at the side of the coffin in tears. My relatives lived in Yorkshire and I had seen very little of them since I was young, so nobody had told me that someone in the family had died. Noting other details, I told my brother what I had been given and he said he had not heard of a death in the family either. He passed the message on to my mother, who immediately telephoned our relatives in Yorkshire. My aunt told her their son had unexpectedly died. They were suffering so badly from shock that they were too traumatised to let any of us know. Once again, the evidence was for someone else.

*

My life became busy with readings, healing and church bookings. I held my own classes at home, as well as teaching and giving lectures for the local Adult Education Institute. At that time this was a very new type of class for them to have on their curriculum.

Although I work on a spiritual level, I have an earthy sense of humour and I prefer to keep both my feet on the ground. On one occasion, a friend and I attended a workshop on colour, music and the psychic faculty. It was a very hot day and the hall had full-length windows, which were opened wide to let in air. The hall backed onto an apartment and from where we stood we could see into the bedroom. The occupants had opened their windows too - and they taken off their clothes! We were in the middle of singing a hymn, when in full view of us the couple began to have sex. They were well aware that they could be seen, especially as they appeared to perform in time to the singing. They were laughing so much that in the end they gave up and pulled their curtains across the window. Those of us in the hall who saw them were in stitches.

Another time, Pete had to make a visit to his accountant in Sheen and I went along to keep him company. While he was sorting out his affairs, two of the women working in the office were chatting to me about my psychic work. Pete's accountant heard us and began to take the "mickey" out of me.

"I suppose you'll be paying me a visit soon, asking me to claim for your long, dangly earrings, crystal ball and scarf," he said laughing.

"You don't want to take the rise out of Ann," Pete joked, "You don't know what she's capable of."

We were still laughing as we left the office.

On the way to the accountant the summer sky had been clear and without a cloud in sight, but as we drove home through Richmond Park, storm clouds began gathering. By the time we got to Kingston, there was heavy rain with thunder and lightening. We knew it would only take about ten minutes to reach Sheen. So, as soon as we were indoors Pete phoned his accountant saying, "Ann wasn't at all happy about your remarks. She's been concentrating hard since we arrived home and within ten minutes or so, you'll find a terrific storm over your building."

Fifteen minutes later his accountant phoned him back. "We've got one hell of storm going on here, thunder, lightening, hail, the whole works."

"Of course you have!" said Pete.

On another occasion I had arranged to visit a fellow medium. When I arrived she appeared hot and flustered.

"What've you been up to?" I asked as I walked through the door.

"Nothing," she said, shaking her head.

Looking at her, I clearly saw in her aura, a picture of a man making love to her. I knew she was separated from her husband, but I was not aware of anyone new in her life.

"You've got yourself a boyfriend," I commented.

"What makes you think that?" she asked.

"I can see him."

"Describe him then?" she said.

After giving the description of her lover, I said with a grin, "And I can see what you've been up to."

Now laughing she said, "Go on then, tell me."

"You were making love in this room. And not long ago either."

"Good guess, but you'll have to come up with more than that."

So I did.

Now blushing, she said, "For Goodness sake, don't say any more!"

We were both laughing as I flippantly imitated Ivy, "Then you'd better cleanse and close, hadn't you."

Because we were both mediums, the energy had been strong, enabling me to see clearly without even trying. However, there is no way that I would tell a sitter something like that, even if I had seen it. Many people seem to think that you only have to look at them and you instantly know everything about them, but this simply isn't true. Generally speaking, unless deliberately working on a psychic level, there is nothing to see. If possible, I prefer to keep my psychic and physical life separate, because it can be depleting to keep going from one level to another.

There is a code of ethics between genuine mediums that says, "unless asked, never invade another person's psychic space." I would not walk into somebody's house without being invited, and neither would I tune into someone without being asked.

As the physical, sexual and psychic energy are one and the same, the more developed the medium, the stronger the energies become. There are many mediums who abstain from sex the day before a sitting, because they believe the energy for the reading will be weakened by making love beforehand. Often marriages break up if one partner becomes involved in the psychic field and the other is not interested. This nearly always happens if one person is sceptical. The sceptic will often demand that the partner gives up the pathway, but usually the medium moves on, instinctively fulfilling his or her destiny.

During my training I decided to study the Tarot cards as another tool to use in a reading. The Tarot has nothing to do with mediumship, but some people have no interest in the after-life, and only want help on a practical level. To me, the cards are very positive, and unless a sitter asks me not to do so, I will always include the Tarot after clairvoyance in a reading. This way, not only do both readings confirm each other, but also the material and spiritual come together.

Obviously, if someone wanted to, they could use their abilities for the purpose of black magic. A very psychic woman once told me that she could not stand her mother-in-law interfering in her life. Whilst visualising her, she made a little doll and stuck a pin into the chest area, before putting it away in a drawer. Within days, she heard that her mother-in-law had suffered a heart attack. Of course, her mother-in-law probably had heart problems before this, but the psychic was terrified that she might have caused it, and that it would rebound back on her in some way.

Win had taught me a little bit about the occult. The word itself simply means "hidden" but people tend to associate it with black magic. Win thought it was important that I learned to recognise some of the negative aspects, in order to protect myself if I should ever find myself in that situation. As the occult is secret, there is not a great deal that one can learn without getting directly involved, for the majority of information given is by word of mouth. Not wanting to go down that pathway, I only took on board the little that Win could teach me about protection.

Spirit had told me on several occasions that I would be taken into different situations, whereby I would use the knowledge gained in my role as a teacher, and black magic was one of those situations. Each time I was asked by someone if they could join my class at home, I would interview them first to see if they were suitable. In this way I could tell how psychic they were, and what direction they were best suited. On one occasion, I was approached by two men and a woman.

"Would you sit in front of me, Dougie, with Barbara over there, and Tom on this side," I said, pointing to chairs, "this will enable me to see into each aura." After tuning into Dougie, I asked him why he wanted to join my class.

"I've heard of your reputation for being a good teacher and I know I'll make a good medium under your guidance," he answered.

Pandering to the teacher will not get you far, I thought as I studied him. As I asked him other questions, I began to feel uncomfortable; I couldn't say why, because superficially everything appeared to be okay. My guide suggested that I took him on as a student, so I dismissed my misgivings as being purely personal.

Tuning in to Tom was the same. His character was not as dominant as Dougie's, but I was still uneasy. Again, my guide told me to ask him to join the class. When it came to Barbara, it was different story. Her aura was full of images of demons and witches.

"You don't need a circle like mine," I told her, "because you're already on the left-hand path and it looks as if you have been for sometime."

"No, you're wrong. I don't know anything about black magic," she replied.

"I can see what you've been up to," I said, "and I don't want people like you in my home."

"Good, we were hoping you would pick that up," said my guide.

By now, Dougie had joined her protest, while Tom sat quietly.

Despite the insistence from my guide that he stayed, I turned to Dougie and said, "Don't take me for a fool. As you feel so strongly, I think it would be better if all three of you left."

"Okay. So she's dabbled a bit. But she's not involved in anything now," he said.

"You took your time admitting that. And, why are you speaking up for her? Can't you speak for yourself, Barbara?"

Nervously, her eyes blinked towards him and back to me. "I'm sorry I didn't say so in the beginning. I thought you wouldn't have me if you knew. I haven't done anything bad. I've only ever showed an interest in it. Honestly."

Looking at her again, I took my energy higher and could see a figure standing behind her. It appeared to be a guide, but there was no light around him. The figure was dressed from head to foot in black robes with a hood pulled across his face.

"Show yourself to me," I commanded.

He didn't answer, nor did he remove the hood from his face.

The voice of my guide was more urgent. "Come away from her, cleanse yourself and tell her again you will not have her in your class, but you must let the other two join."

"I'm not wasting anymore time. I'll take you and Tom but Barbara has to go," I told them.

Jumping up, Dougie said, "Oh, thanks, Ann. We'll see you next week then. Come on, you two, it's time to leave."

Without another word, Tom and Barbara quickly followed him towards the door.

Then Barbara stopped, turning back to face me. She had a smirk on her mouth and I thought she was going to say something. However, she just shuffled out behind the others, slamming the door on the way.

"Why is it so important to have them in my class?" I asked my guide.

"It is necessary for your own development, child, and you will find out soon enough."

The following week, a few minutes before the start of my class I opened the door to find Dougie, Tom and Barbara on my doorstep. They followed each other in, until I reached out to stop Barbara. "Where do you think you're going?"

"Upstairs, with the others," she responded.

"What on earths the matter with you? When I said I didn't want you, I meant it."

Dougie stopped in his tracks and they both stared at each other, before he nodded and she turned and walked out.

There's something very weird going on here, I thought, as I followed him upstairs.

After introducing them to the other students, I explained what we were going to do.

"I know all about that," Dougie remarked.

Cathy interrupted, "If you know so much, why are you in Ann's class?"

Oh God, here we go. He's already rubbing the others up the wrong way, I thought. This class is not going to work with these vibes.

"We'll begin by you all tuning into Tom. So, Tom, if you'll just relax, someone will come to you when they're ready."

Only one of my students came up with some kind of a message for him. None of the others had anything to say, including Cathy, who at that time was my best student. I found myself turning towards her, wondering why she was silent. She was certainly tuning in because I could see her doing it. I had told Pete about Dougie and Tom, and asked him to sit in with us. After the class, I wanted his thoughts and opinion of them. The circle didn't go well and I was glad when it was time to finish.

I was watching to see if everyone was closing down correctly, when I noticed that Tom was swaying.

"Tom, are you okay?" I asked.

He opened his eyes and looked at me. "Yeah, I'm fine."

"Are you having a job closing down?"

"No, I don't think so."

"Well, I would rather you tried again, because something's not right."

Watching him closely, I could see that he was trying to close his crown chakra. Each time he made the effort, he swayed and the chakra came open again.

"I've already explained that the crown centre stays open, along with the base of the spine. You're trying to close it off and it's making you unsteady."

He turned to Dougie who answered for him. "We believe that the crown chakra should be closed."

"It's left open for your spiritual development, Dougie, so if you try to close it, you'll fall over. However, you obviously know best."

He shrugged his shoulders and looked away.

The class broke up but before Cathy left she said, "I'm sorry, Ann, but if you keep them in this class I'm leaving. They both work for the other side and I don't want anything to do with it."

"Cathy, I want you here because I need someone as good as you to observe what's going on. You're right. Both of them are involved with the left-hand path, but I've been told by my guide it's important for me to include them for the time being. You know nothing will happen to you. We'll all be protected and you could learn something from this yourself."

"No. I'm sorry to let you down, but I have my children to think of and I can't risk it." She left, and I was sad to see her go. She was one of the best students I had ever had, and she would be a brilliant medium. Pete and I discussed what had happened. Neither of us was happy about the situation, but we decided to leave it in the hands of spirit.

At the following week's meeting, Dougie was more dominant. It looked as though Tom was subservient to him, because he always turned to Dougie for answers. Dougie had ideas of his own that he was determined to implement, so he brought up the subject of Jesus and the Devil.

"Jesus had twelve disciples and some of us here have the same initials. Jill for Jesus, Peter the Fisherman, Doubting Thomas, Ann for Andrew and Sue for Simon. Maybe you're his disciples reincarnated."

"You've a vivid imagination, Dougie. Where do you come into all of this with the letter D?"

"Could be I'm a reincarnation of the Devil."

"Mmm, and could be you're talking a load of old twaddle. Now, let's get down to the reason why you're here."

As the class ended, I overheard him talking to one of the other students.

"I want to set up a group of my own, and you would be perfect for it," he said.

"No. I'm not interested," answered the student.

He approached all the students in turn and asked the same question, and each one turned him down. Then he began to discuss the reasons as to why the sexual act could be a positive power in a psychic group.

"Time to go home now," I interrupted him in mid-flow, "see you next week."

He gave me this funny little grin, coupled with the same gleam in his eyes that I had first seen in Barbara's.

Turning, he called out, "Okay. See you all next week."

That left three of us – Pete, me and Jill, who was a close friend of ours.

"Well, what do you both think of him?" I asked as soon as I closed the door.

"It's pretty obvious that he's here to poach your students for his own group," Pete answered.

"Yeah, but he doesn't want to develop them in the same way," I said thoughtfully. "I'm not going to have him back here again. I think he could be dangerous. He was coming on pretty strong to you tonight, Jill."

"I know. He wanted my telephone number. He said he wanted to take me out."

"Did you give it to him?"

"No I didn't. He's pretty weird. I told him I was married and not interested in going out with him. Nevertheless, I have to say I thought he was mesmerising. When I looked into his eyes, I found it difficult to turn away."

"You were the only one who thought so. None of the others had a problem with turning him down, so I would not be surprised if he latches onto you; be careful. I'm going to ring him tomorrow and tell him not to come back again."

We agreed it was the best thing to do and I felt relieved that I had made a decision.

The following day I phoned him. "Dougie? It's Ann. I've decided I can't have you in my class any more. It isn't working out."

"You said it would be okay for Tom and me to come providing we left Barbara out of it. So why've you changed your mind?"

"The class isn't gelling. The vibrations aren't right, and Barbara's still very much on the scene. Not that I'm telling you whom you can or cannot see, but the influences around you are dark and not conducive to my teaching."

"Oh, okay. If that's the way you want it. But before I go, could you give me Jill's telephone number?"

"No. I won't give out any telephone numbers without permission."

"Well, can you ask her for me?"

"No. I'm sure that if Jill wanted you to have it, she would have given it to you before now."

"You bloody cow," he shouted. "I'll get you for this."

Taken aback by his outburst, I slowly replaced the receiver. As I walked away it rang again. Hesitating slightly, I turned and lifted it once more to my ear.

"Ann. It's Tom. I need to get in touch with Jill. Will you please let me have her number?"

I told him, "Dougie must be desperate, if he's got you asking me – and no - you can't have it, but I'll pass on a message if you want me to."

He put down the telephone.

That evening when I tuned in to my guide, I received a telling off.

"It is unfortunate you decided to take this action. As this lesson has been terminated, we will have to begin again."

"What have I done?" I asked inwardly, "I recognised that Dougie was on the wrong pathway and wanted our knowledge for his own gain. If he'd stayed, I would have lost all of my students."

"You did not handle the situation correctly. You should have confronted him with the truth. It was necessary to make him aware that you knew what he was doing. Now, child, you will be taken along that pathway again, and there will be more to contend with the next time. You must learn to recognise the sign of evil so that you can deal with it should you find yourself in that position." His voice was still soft and gentle, but there was no mistaking the strength behind it.

17
The Devil Rides In

"If you would like to make an appointment, June, we'll have a chat to see if you're suitable for my circle."

"Would it be possible for you to come to me?" she asked, "I don't live very far from you."

"I don't normally travel out to see people - the student usually comes to me for the interview."

"Can you make an exception this time? I have to keep an eye on the house next door, and I don't know when I'll be able to leave it."

Pausing for a moment, I picked up the pen and said, "Okay. Give me your address."

Her house was in a private road, in a very select part of Kingston.

"I'll see you in half an hour, Ann. I'm looking forward to meeting you."

As it happened, I did have some free time. It was a beautiful day and it would be nice to get out of the house for a while. Within ten minutes I had found the road, and as I drove through the private gates, I entered another world. I glimpsed palatial houses set back from the road, surrounded by trees in stunning gardens. Driving slowly, I peered from side to side, not wanting to miss the house. At first I thought I had, when finally, almost at the other end of the road, I saw the sign half hidden by trees. Turning into the drive, I parked the car and made my way to the door. Knocking several times brought no response, so after a few minutes I gave up.

I went back to my car, wrote a short note to say I had been and popped it through her letterbox. Then I drove home.

I could hear my 'phone ringing as I turned the key in the door, and I ran to answer it. Before I could open my mouth, I heard June apologising.

"I'm so sorry I missed you, Ann. I was next door checking that everything was okay with the house. Please say you'll come back and have a coffee with me."

The urge to say no was uppermost, but I told her I would drive over again. I must be mad, I thought as I made my way back to the car.

"No, child," a soft voice sounded inside my head. "It is important to keep this engagement and to do exactly what we ask of you."

With my head full of questions, I turned once again into her drive and saw a small, dark haired woman standing in front of the door. She waved at me and ran towards my car as I pulled up.

"Ann?" asked the woman.

"Yes. And you must be June."

She nodded and apologised again, while at the same time glancing at her watch.

We were about to go into the house when a pale blue sports car with the top down, came speeding into the drive. It came screeching to a halt, sending gravel flying in all directions. Behind the wheel was a middle-aged blond woman talking and laughing loudly to her only passenger, a younger woman with auburn hair.

June turned towards them and said, "Ann, meet Rachel and Pauline. I've told them all about you. When they knew you were coming over, Rachel asked if she could meet you in the hope she could also join your class."

There's something peculiar going on here, I thought. With the mix up over the times, how did they know when I would arrive? June must have phoned them shortly after speaking to me.

My guide answered my unspoken question. "It is important that you follow this through."

Whilst June busied herself making coffee, we sat down at the kitchen table. Rachel was loud, and she didn't stop yakking from the moment that we had walked through the door. She was now reliving the events of a shopping trip to a jewellery shop. The owner of the shop knew her very well, it seemed, and he had apparently noted the absence of her bra.

"You're flaunting it today, darling, but if you're going to flaunt it – then flaunt it," he told her, putting a hand inside her blouse and pulling her breast out onto the counter top.

To emphasise the point, she lifted out her well-endowed right boob and laid it on the kitchen table.

Here I was; sitting with three women I had only met a few minutes ago, with one of them laying her naked assets between me and the coffee cups. Taken by surprise, I wasn't sure how to react to this. The others were laughing but Rachel kept glancing at me. I felt she was deliberately trying to shock me and that she was looking for a reaction. She had succeeded. Going along with it, I smiled at her, while making up my mind there was no way this woman was coming into my class.

I heard my guide speaking. "You will invite her to join your class. It is important. Pauline will not join and June will only stay for a short while. But you must still ask them to come."

So I went along with it. Arrangements were made for them to meet up with me and the rest of the class at Seymour Place in London, where a friend was lending us the use of her house.

From the beginning, Rachel was trouble. She messed around in class, telling jokes and laughing hysterically. I always placed her opposite me so that I could see her clearly.

Whenever we opened up in prayer, she would be looking around the room or sitting with her arms folded and her legs crossed. She seemed to get on well with the other students, even though none of them ever gave her clairvoyance. Whenever I tuned into her, I saw darkness and a guide dressed in black robes with a hood pulled across his face. This scenario seems familiar, I thought, remembering back to the Barbara incident, but despite the way things were looking, I couldn't get any answers to my questions from my guide.

We had not been using Seymour Place for long when Rachel asked me if we could hold the class at her home in Kingston. "I've a huge house, plenty of room and as most of us live in or around Kingston, it makes sense. Who wants to spend time travelling this far, to use this poky room when we could all be more comfortable at my place."

I could not think of any good reason to refuse her offer, so I reluctantly agreed. I wanted to make sure the room in her home was suitable for our needs, so I asked her if I could come round first before arranging to hold the class there. A few days later, I was invited to join her for coffee, and with some trepidation, I found myself driving up to her door. Rachel had said her home was huge and this was no exaggeration. It was sitting in magnificent grounds, with a smaller house to one side and further buildings dotted around.

Rachel was watching out for me and she opened the door before I could ring the bell. Stepping into the hallway, I could hear chatter and laughter drifting out from somewhere deeper in the house. As I followed her, I glanced at a painting on the wall. It was a picture of nuns standing beside the ruins of a church. It was a night-time scene, and each nun had a skull instead of a face peering out from beneath her cowl. A shiver ran through me, as I wondered who in their right mind would want a painting of skeletons on her wall.

In the kitchen, I was greeted by several noisy people who continued talking to each other. After sitting down at the table, I looked around and recognised Pauline but there was no sign of June. Two women had their arms wrapped around each other and appeared to be whispering sweet nothings, whilst an effeminate man leaning against the wall was calling out advice to Pauline from across the room.

"You've done the right thing coming home, Pauline darling. After living in Saudi with those horrible louts pawing you, this must seem heavenly. Oh yuck, I could easily throw up thinking about it." Lifting his hand he waved it limply before wiping it across his brow.

"Think of the money, that's what counts," Rachel shouted as she turned to Pauline, "and you must have made a bomb, the amount of blokes you had."

"Yeah, but I couldn't walk after a month, so I knew it was time to call it a day."

The conversation carried on along those lines.

It was clear that Pauline was a prostitute and that she had been invited to Saudi Arabia for that purpose. However, while she was there, one of her rich clients gave her a beating, and that is the real reason she had come back to England.

The two women were now kissing each other, oblivious to everyone else.

Although I was drinking coffee with them, I was not really included in the conversation and I wondered if any of this was for my benefit. It was all pretty sordid and it became even more so when Rachel was asked about her husband.

"Are you still feeding him cat food?"

"Only if he's been a good boy. When he's on the lead, he has to crawl around the kitchen first before he can have it."

"You're talking about the cat food I presume," laughed Pauline.

"Both, if he's really good. Ron caught us at it the other day. There I was, all dressed up in rubber, whip in hand with Moggy bending over, when suddenly he appeared through the door and scared the living daylights out of me."

"What did he do when he saw you?"

"Took his clothes off and joined in."

Their screams of laughter bounced off the walls and I laughed along with them.

It was hard to believe this could be real, but my instincts told me that it was. I stood up and asked Rachel if she would show me the room she wanted us to use for the circle. Everyone followed us out and we trooped up the stairs and into a large, sunny room at the back of the house.

"I thought this would be perfect," Rachel said, "and I've got more chairs if we need them."

As I crossed the threshold, a chill ran up my spine and my skin broke out in goose bumps. On the surface everything looked okay, but I recognised from so long ago the old feeling of dread connected with unwanted spirits.

"Someone has died in this room," I blurted out.

"Yeah, they did. Would that make a difference, then?"

"Not if they died naturally, but this was a suicide and that'll make a big difference."

"In what way?" asked Rachel.

"Often a suicide carries into spirit the conditions with which he left the earth. This may well have happened here. If so, the atmosphere will be negative and it will be difficult to raise the vibrations above it."

"A friend of mine took an overdose and was found dead in here. Surely someone like him couldn't cause that much of a problem?"

"It wasn't just him. There were two others, and they both died from taking drugs. It's too risky to hold a developing class under those conditions."

Rachel was staring at me with her mouth open.

"That is what happened, isn't it?"

Quickly regaining her composure, she nodded. "There's only the dining room left," she said, brushing past me and out through the door.

Once again, we all followed her as she made her way down the stairs and along the hall. Further on I noted another painting on the opposite wall, depicting a similar scene of skeletons dressed as nuns. All of my senses were wide-awake, as I realised I was getting deeper and deeper into a situation that was connected with black magic.

"Don't be nervous, child. You are doing well. We are here to protect you and we will not let you down."

The gentle voice of my guide was clear in my head as I entered the dining room. Directly opposite me, hanging on the wall, was another painting. This time it was the Devil. Feeling someone watching me, I turned to see Rachel glance away with a small grin on her face. My instinct was to walk out but once more I heard the voice of my guide.

"Stay. It is important. You will come to no harm. This room should be used."

Breathing deeply, I looked around. "The atmosphere is better in here," I told Rachel. "It will be fine, but only on the condition that you remove that painting while we hold the class. It's not exactly conducive to spiritual development."

Nodding my head towards the picture of the Devil, I could swear the eyes followed my movement.

"Okay, if that's what you want," said Rachel.

We made arrangements to meet the following week, along with the other students. I then made my excuses and left.

*

Discussing the position with Pete later that evening, I asked him if he wanted to come to the class with me.

"None of the students are aware of what is going on. Although I've been told by spirit over and over again to do what is asked, I feel guilty leading the students into such a negative situation."

"There wouldn't be any point in having me there," he replied, "my clairvoyance isn't as good as yours."

Thinking for a moment he said, "What you need is someone like yourself, who can verify everything."

"I know! Dolly. I'll ask her. She'll be perfect."

Dolly was my friend Dorothy Chapman from our own development class. We had often worked together and her mediumship was good, so I knew I could rely on her. Pete thought she was the right choice – especially, as like me, she ran her own classes. After phoning and explaining what I was involved with, Dolly didn't hesitate. None of my students had met her before, so we agreed that I would tell them she was simply sitting in the class for the experience.

As we pulled up outside Rachel's house the following week, we could see other vehicles parked close by. I recognised most of them as belonging to members of my own group. The door had been left open for us to walk right in. I had mentioned the paintings to Dolly, so I was not surprised to see her looking at them closely as we walked through the hallway.

"They're weird, but they don't frighten me," she whispered.

We made our way through to the dining room and saw that the painting of the Devil was still in place. Rachel had set out the chairs in a circle and was seated and chatting to one of the girls. She glanced up at me and smirked. I was about to speak to her, but the other students followed me in and there was a lot of chatter and dragging of chairs as they sorted themselves out.

"Do not worry about the painting, it cannot hurt you, child," a familiar voice reassured me.

Sitting in the chair facing the picture felt uncomfortable. I had a strong sense of the portrait willing me to look at it.

Determined to ignore it, I asked Dolly to sit several seats away on my right, before asking Rachel to sit opposite me. She willingly moved and the room gradually became quiet as everyone settled.

"Would you open in prayer, Rachel?" I asked.

"Oh no, do I have to? I wouldn't know what to say."

"What about the Lord's Prayer. Surely you know that?"

"I'll say it if everyone joins in with me."

"Okay. Are you all ready?" I asked the group.

Nods and mumbles answered me, as they closed their eyes. Staring at Rachel, I watched closely as she appeared to join in with the others. It didn't take long to become aware that she seemed to be reciting the prayer backwards. You would expect this from a Dennis Wheatley book, I thought, but not in real life.

After saying Amen, I asked the class to tune into Rachel while I took my own energy higher. Behind her, I could see the same figure as before, dressed from head to foot in black, with a cowl drawn across the face. Darkness still surrounded him. "You're in my class, so show yourself to me," I inwardly told the figure. The head slowly lifted, and I had the impression of eyes staring through me. Then a fleshless hand whipped the hood away, exposing the head of a skeleton. "Some guide you've got, woman, nothing but a bag of bones," was the sarcastic thought I sent to them.

This appeared to enrage her guide, as it lunged across the circle to me. However, it was flung back as it came in contact with the huge band of light that encircled all of us with the exception of Rachel. The skeleton gave a bellow of pain, and tried once more to get to me through the band of light. Several times it was knocked back as it stretched out its skeletal fingers to touch me.

"Get back to your own squalid level," I shouted with my mind. "You don't have the ability to break through the power of light. You're too pathetic."

To my astonishment he returned to stand behind Rachel. The cowl was drawn across his face and the hand of bone changed to flesh. Dropping my gaze from him, I looked at the class. We were still encased in a band of gold light that was at least four foot in height and which ran in a complete circle behind everyone. Although Rachel was still sitting in the same position, somehow the light entirely missed her.

"You must close the circle down now, my child. You have done well so far, but do not confront her here on her own ground. You must return home and use the telephone to speak with her."

I thanked him before saying to the students, "I know Rachel isn't easy to tune into, but did anyone manage to get any information from her?"

One or two said that they had not and the others shook their heads.

"As you've had difficulty tuning in tonight, I'm going to cut the session short. You've tried hard, I know, and you will no doubt feel depleted, but there is no point in continuing if it isn't working. It's probably because we're using this room for the first time, and it will take some getting used to. So Dolly, would you close in prayer for me?"

Several students were yawning. I knew why they were depleted. Their energies had been diverted to help build the circle of protection. Naturally, they were unaware of this, and I could see that I would have some explaining to do later. Once the class was over, we said goodnight and followed each other outside. Sitting in my car, I turned to Dolly and asked her what she had seen.

"There was a huge figure dressed in black standing with Rachel. He suddenly moved and threw off his hood, but I could not believe what I was seeing. It was a skeleton. It was trying to get at you, but spirit had built a barrier of light around everybody, and it couldn't get through."

"That's exactly what I saw," I said with relief. "I'm so pleased you came tonight, because if I'd told this to anyone else they'd have said I was nuts."

"It was incredible. I've never come across anything like this before," she said, "and what's more Ann, she's well and truly involved in the black arts. I was picking up all kinds of things with her. I saw her out in the woods somewhere with other people, all of them dressed up in long cloaks and dancing around a big fire. Then I was shown a baby and I felt sure it was going to be used as some kind of sacrifice because I had a terrible feeling connected with it."

Driving home, I knew that it was important to phone Rachel as soon as I could. However, I decided to leave it until the following day, because I needed to hear advice from my guide before I took any action.

"Rachel will not accept that she cannot return to your class. She needed the energy from your students for her own purposes, and would have tried to take them from you. It is important that you tell her exactly what you have seen. She will scream, shout and use abusive language. You must use a psychic protection around your home and family because she will try to send dark forces to you. We will help you to counteract this."

That night I used the psychic protection ritual that Win had taught me so that I could ensure that I already had something in place before I made my phone call. The following morning I rang her.

"Rachel? It's Ann. I'll no longer be using your house for teaching, nor do I want you anymore in my class."

"Why? What on earth have I done?"

"You're fully aware of what's been going on, Rachel. You're well and truly involved in black magic, and I will not expose my students or myself to it any longer."

"That's a load of rubbish. Is it because I left that painting on the wall?"

"That didn't help, but it was obvious from the guide that you have with you, along with the company that you keep. There are other reasons, too. That "thing" you call a guide, was evil. And you loved every moment, taunting me, not thinking for one minute that I would do anything about it."

There was silence and I thought she had gone, when suddenly she began shouting and swearing at me. This lasted about a minute before the line went dead.

Immediately, I contacted all of my students and arranged to meet them again in London, and I told them that I would explain everything to them when we met.

Later that evening, I sat in my quiet room and tuned into spirit. "She did exactly as you said she would, lots of threats and swearing. Although I know this test was mainly for my benefit, how is it going to change her life?"

"It is not possible for you to change her pathway. You can only show her enlightenment. She decided on this before she was born to this world. Every spirit chooses the lessons it needs to evolve spiritually, and this was her choice," he answered.

As predicted, June had not turned up for many of my classes, but the following day I received a phone call from her inviting Pete and me to meet her husband Michael. She added that there were a few things she wanted us to know about Rachel. This could be interesting, I thought, as I accepted her invitation for the following week.

My psychic protection was placed firmly around everyone, plus the house and car, for several weeks. Although we had a few restless nights at the start, nothing worrying occurred.

*

"Thank God you saw through her so quickly, I was worried sick about your students," June said. "That's the reason I didn't turn up for the classes. I was concerned that you wouldn't be able to handle it."

"At least you're being honest," I replied.

"The kind of people Rachel mixes with leaves a lot to be desired," Michael butted in, "and at times I've told June she would do well to stay away from her."

June gave him an old-fashioned look before turning back to me. "That magnificent house she lives in; well, that's paid for by social services. Don't ask me how she gets away with it. Her husband is a declared bankrupt and she said the house is going to be put up for sale. That was months ago, but there's no sign of it yet."

"Tell Ann and Pete about Moggy," Michael said with a laugh.

"Well, they're both into the kinky stuff, handcuffs, leather, whips, you name it and they've done it. She entertains rich Arab men and Moggy knows all about it. That's because they pay good money, and he reaps the benefit."

"Is it true about the cat food? Does she really make him eat it?" I asked.

"Oh yes, it's all true. I've seen it. She makes him walk on a lead, and then he has to beg before she allows him near it."

"Ann said they were talking about all of this when she went round to the house that day for coffee, but she thought it was put on a bit for her benefit."

"Pete, believe me, it's not put on. One morning, they were having sex and Moggy had tied Rachel to the bed, but they ended up having a row. He was so uptight that he walked out and left her there, still tied up. She had nothing on, and it was only because the window cleaner saw her that afternoon that she managed to get free. If he hadn't, she would have been stuck there for hours, because Moggy didn't come home until the following evening."

Pete was laughing, "And I suppose she wouldn't feed him his Kitty-Kat after that!"

"We may well think it's funny, but she's been into some really bad stuff," Michael said. "They've always taken drugs and her sixteen year old son is an addict. He's currently living at the top of the house with his sixteen year old girl friend who is about to have a baby."

My stomach flipped. Dolly had seen a baby whom she thought was going to be used as a sacrifice. I told them about this.

"I wouldn't put it past her," Michael remarked.

"Her son has been trying to find somewhere else to live," June said. "He wants to leave the drugs behind him, but Rachel is constantly on hand with more. He wants to get out before the baby is born. Maybe he's aware that something is going on, because Rachel is practically begging him to stay until after the birth, even offering him the smaller house to live in."

I had been wondering why June was involved with Rachel, especially knowing how dangerous she could be. As we were preparing to leave she said, "I haven't been round to see Rachel for ages, and I've no intention of getting in touch with her again. We've put our house on the market and we're moving far away, so she can't get her claws into me again."

It was obvious that Rachel had had some kind of hold over June, and that June was frightened of her. So frightened, that she felt the only way to be free of her clutches was to move house, which Michael agreed to do.

She telephoned a few weeks later to say the sale of their house had gone through quickly, and they had bought another property nearer the coast. "Rachel has been to my home several times, but I've refused to speak to her. And - some good news, Ann - her son and his girl friend came around to tell me they were moving into a flat well away from his mother. And he's entered a rehabilitation program."

I was pleased she was moving away, because I think Rachel would have done her best to draw June back into her life again. There was no doubt in my mind that spirit had used June for the valuable lesson that I had to learn in recognising evil. At the same time June had found the strength to break away from Rachel, and hopefully, so had Rachel's son. As for me, I hoped I would never have to face another lesson like that again.

18

Clients and Others

The following week, I explained to my students what had happened. "There was never any danger to any of you," I told them, "but if I'd told you what I was doing, there would have been a chance that one of you would have inadvertently let it slip out." They asked several questions and I was completely honest with them, explaining exactly what Dolly and I had experienced and how spirit had guided me through the whole situation.

After the Rachel incident, life settled down a little and I concentrated once more on my psychic work. Despite the fact that spirit guided me most of the time, I was aware that I could not simply sit back and wait for someone to tell me what to do. It was necessary for me to do things for myself, and if I made mistakes, I had to learn from them. Usually my students were guided to me, but at one point my beginners' class had finished and I had not received any new inquiries. So I took it upon myself to advertise in the local paper. After placing the advert, my guide told me I should stop working for a while, as it was important for me to have a rest from teaching. There were several replies to my advert, and defiantly, I ignored his advice and went ahead with the interviews. But spirit thought differently.

"Each student will leave your class for various reasons. You need a rest. If you are tired or unwell, your mediumship will suffer. We will always guide people to you. If people do not come to you, child, it will be for a reason."

Still defiant, I carried on. By the fourth week, all eight students had left, and every time this was due to happen, my guide had told me which one it would be. Despite knowing my destiny had been mapped out for me, I had always felt it important to exert my own free will along my pathway. In this instance, though, spirit knew best, as shortly afterwards I was unwell and unable to work for a while. Since then, I have discovered that if work didn't come my way, it was always for a good reason, and I have learnt to accept this.

*

After giving a private reading, I always stress that there is no need for the sitter to have another one for at least six months. Of course, there are exceptions, but generally speaking, a good reading will not change much over the following year. However, there are some people who get hooked on the psychic scene, almost to the exclusion of anything else in their lives. One such person was a young woman named Lynne.

"I can see you with two more children," I said.

"They can't be my children then, because I can't have any more."

"They are your children, I'm certain of that," I said, "I'm not being told whether you will become pregnant yourself or if you're adopting them, only that they're yours."

"I'm going through a difficult time with my partner, so I certainly won't be adopting any. Perhaps they belong to a friend?" asked Lynne.

"No, they're yours. No question about it. And you'll be entering a new relationship soon, so the opportunity could well arise."

"Now look, Ann, there's no way I would want to adopt and I can't have any more children. I've had several ectopic pregnancies, leaving me with one blocked fallopian tube and only half of the other one. My specialist told me I would never conceive again. So you must have got your wires crossed."

Lynne was so adamant that I didn't pursue it. I gave her further information from my guide concerning her family and then finished the reading.

"Can I make another appointment for next month?" she asked.

"We've already discussed this, Lynne. You should not need to see me so often. I've not given you anything different in this reading to what I gave you last month. You're only wasting your money."

"That's fine with me. I like to have confirmation on what you've given me before."

"I've just confirmed the two children, but you won't accept what spirit is giving you, because you think it's impossible for it to happen. I suggest you leave it for at least three months before getting in touch with me again."

So she left, but she was not happy at having to wait for three months. She had been coming to me for a year, but the readings didn't vary much now, and I was beginning to remember them too.

Exactly three months later, Lynne booked another appointment. The reading was much the same. I could see her with a baby girl, and at a later date with a baby boy. There was further information, though, about another relationship.

"In a few weeks there will be a new relationship for you, which I know will make you happy," I said.

"I hope so. I've had enough of men to last a lifetime - so this one had better be good!

"Listen to me, Lynne. I'm not going to see you for another year. You can't go on like this. When you come again, you'll still be with this new man and you can then tell me I was right."

That didn't stop her phoning to tell me how things were. Every time she socialised, she would look to see if there was a man fitting the description I had given her. It didn't matter whether he was married or not, she would home in on the poor guy until, for one reason or another, she found he wasn't the right one. However, a few months after our last sitting, she told me she was involved with someone looking exactly as I had described. After that I didn't hear from her for a while, so eventually she faded to the back of my mind. Two years passed before she got in touch again. I felt sure there would be something new to tell her, so I was looking forward to her visit.

"Spirit's telling me you have settled down with the man I said you would meet. I have a picture of you laughing and I can see you both with a baby girl. My guide is showing her as a little older than before – about four months, I think. She's your baby, isn't she?"

"Yes. You were right. The doctors don't know how it's happened. They said it should have been impossible, but I have conceived. She's nearly four months old and absolutely beautiful."

The clairvoyant picture I saw showed me that she was gorgeous. Against all the odds, there must be a good reason why this baby had been meant to be born. Continuing with the reading, I found that Lynne had developed her own latent psychic ability, and I was told she would be in the public eye. First there would be an article in the newspaper and then she would appear on local television. She was more settled in her personal life now, so she didn't feel the need to come and see me that often. As time passed, she had another baby - a boy - and she became well-known in the media for her psychic work.

19

An Angelic Meeting

All words die and everything dies
and all in silence and cold,
Stuff of death and the sarcophagus.
In the full light shining, a river runs,
far from the stoniness,
And hardened by gloom, the snow, falling,
Takes itself off from dying and dies as it falls
From the cruel heights where it was sleeping;
Yesterday, shrouded today,
Lover of the wind.
Pablo Neruda

Sitting in my "quiet" room one afternoon, I reflected upon how far I had travelled along the psychic pathway that was to be my destiny. Although it appeared to me that my journey had only begun a few months before, it had actually been happening all my life. Even if I had wanted to, I couldn't have changed things. I had tried in the past, and had been brought back to that same pathway time and again. As I considered some of the readings I had given, I was filled with a sense of awe at the way spirit had used me to give hope, guidance and love to those in need. There was a time when I had thought that maybe I was in some way picking up knowledge from my sitters. However, so much had happened that could not be explained. I had been taught to ask our spirit friends for information from the past and present and then to give me something for the future. There were many times that sitters came back to me to say the future events had happened. This was impossible for me to predict without the intervention of some higher intelligence. I thought how difficult and frustrating it must be for the spirits to get their messages through from one dimension to another by using a bridge like myself to achieve it.

My body was suddenly racked with a spiritual pain of longing. I yearned to be with my spirit friends rather than here on the earth. In that moment of realisation, there was no doubt in my mind that I was only on loan in this physical world, and my home, my real home, was with them. There were no thoughts of suicide: I was not unhappy. I was a messenger, sent out to do a job; and although in that instant I missed my home, I knew that when my job was over I would return, for the essence of all life is eternal.

On a personal level, I had found the pathway difficult, and the sadness I encountered from my sitters upset me. Their tears often flowed, but when someone close to them communicated from spirit, it would make up a little for their heartache. My own sensitivity was difficult to contend with, but without it, I couldn't do this work. Somehow I had learned to cope. My reward came from spirit. I trusted them. They have never let me down, although the same cannot be said of me.

*

I have often been asked why mediums nearly always have Indian or Chinese guides. This is because they each represent the religion or spirituality of their country. Other religions come through too. I have a Bishop, a Spanish nun, Arab and Egyptian guides, to name but a few. My Chinese Mandarin is shown in the most beautiful robes of emerald green and gold, but my Native American Indian wears a simple white outfit wrapped around his body, with one end of the material over his shoulder. In contrast, my Bishop is dressed resplendently in gold and white, from the top of his mitre to the edge of his raiment.

Death brings everyone together. Spirit has no religion, only pure spirituality. Whichever pathway we walk, our destiny is the same. We all return to our birthplace. They have shown me that we live on after we die and that the most important aspect in our lives is love. Love in this world and the next. It is because of the love they bring that I have always thought of my guides and helpers as my Angels.

Traditionally, Angels are depicted in the classic form of having wings. Mine certainly didn't, and neither did I expect to see them that way. I think in my heart, I didn't believe in winged Angels, and although I had an open mind, I kept both feet firmly on the ground. One special evening changed those views forever.

For some time, I had been working with Win and Ivy in a small way. I would stand in for Ivy if she couldn't run her class, or I would get together with Win for a colour, music and psychic demonstration. One summer evening, Win and I held a special event in a small hall at the SAGB. In preparation, we had placed candles around the room and soft music was playing in the background. Between us, we had worked out a program, with Win using music and colour, and me working on a psychic level. The hall was packed, and we had to turn some people away, as we needed room to walk between each person. The session was going well, and after an hour it began to get dark. The candles gave off more than enough light, and we didn't want to use the overhead lamps, as they would spoil the atmosphere. As I moved between the chairs, I noted that each person had his or her eyes closed and appeared to be totally relaxed.

Slowly, I became aware of a golden radiance filling the room. In some surprise I looked up. Before me was the most beautiful being I had ever seen. He was tall, and stood with his head slightly bowed. His eyes were closed and his hands were clasped in prayer. The radiance emanated from him, touching every one of us. His face was exquisite with fine delicate features. A narrow, silver band was threaded through his wavy, dark-blonde hair, whilst the light formed a golden halo behind his head.

I glanced over to Win, but she was looking down, concentrating on her paperwork. I expected him to have vanished when I turned back, but he was still there, and looking as physically substantial as the rest of us.

He wore a long, white robe that ended just above his silver sandals. The robe was edged in silver braid around the neck, sleeves and hem; and a wide, silver belt was clasped around his waist. From his back grew two enormous wings. So large they were only inches from the floor. His feathers were brilliant white, with blue shadows between the folds. He was absolutely stunning. He stirred the most incredible, spiritual emotions within me, and yet I could find no words to describe them. I knew without doubt that I was in the presence of a celestial being of the highest order.

Turning again to Win, I could see she was still sorting through her papers. I threaded my way towards her and touched her hand. She looked up at me and I nodded towards the Angel.

"Can you see the figure across the room?" I whispered.

Following my gaze she said, "Oh my God, he's so beautiful. He's an Angel in the purest form."

We watched him for a few more moments, but gradually he became misty until he and the light disappeared.

After the class ended, not one of the students mentioned our Angel, so we both knew he was only there for our benefit. Neither of us said very much on the way home, each of us was locked in our own thoughts, and it was several days before I told Pete. I did not want to talk about it. I wanted to keep it to myself. It was for me. I felt that by talking about what I had seen would in some way lower the reverence I felt. For some reason, spirit had bestowed a great honour on Win and me. Perhaps my guides wanted me to know that they, too, had Angels guiding them.

20
A Death and a Birth

This is the beginning, not the end, of Life's eternal chain,
For memory will rise up anew, to greet sad day again.
This is the beginning, not the end, though sorrow is unfurled,
For tears are but a speck upon the canvas of the world.
This is the beginning, not the end, like the beauty of a rose,
That fades and is reborn again,
Then even stronger grows.

Anon

When someone approached me for healing, I would normally direct the person to Pete, because he was good at it. However, one day, a woman who lived on our estate asked if I would give her healing for her eyes. Although we weren't friends, I had known Lee when we were children at school, and she had always worn a patch over one eye. A small tube at the back of her left eye had been defective since birth, and although she no longer wore a patch, her vision was impaired. Lee had accepted this problem long ago, as specialists at Moorefield's Eye Hospital had told her that there was nothing they could do to remedy the matter. Despite this she could drive, but she was now having a problem with her right eye, and it was this that she was worried about.

"I can't guarantee that the healing will work, although you should feel better," I told her.

"I'm desperate and I'll try anything to see if it helps. I don't know what I'll do if I can't drive any more."

We made arrangements for her to come to see me once a week for six weeks. Any significant improvement would show during this period.

When she turned up for her first session, I told her that I would need to get to her head and her back, so I asked her to sit sideways on the chair. "Try to relax," I told her.

Placing one hand in front of her right eye and one at the back of her head, I asked inwardly for spirit to help me with healing. My hands were becoming hot and I asked her if she could feel anything.

"Yes, heat. I can feel heat on the back of my head."

"If you feel it's too much, let me know and I'll stop."

I was aware of spirit with me, but because I wanted to concentrate on healing, I didn't ask any questions or try to see who it was. After fifteen minutes, I wanted to move my hands down her spine where I could still feel the energy flowing through my hands. Gradually my hands began to cool and I knew the session was over. Before she left, I advised her to rest at home for a while to allow the healing to work within her. During the second session, my right hand began to tingle, and again I could feel the energy passing from me and into her head. When we were finished, Lee said she thought the healing had been stronger. Although she was not aware of any other sensation, my hands had given off more heat. She assured me that she would lie down for a while at home. She told me she had an appointment that week for her usual check-up at Moorefield's Hospital on the damaged eye. Because of this, we arranged another healing session for the following week.

Lee called in to see me before her appointment, and she was looking very excited. "My specialist has told me that the defective tube at the back of my left eye has somehow made a connection, giving some enhancement to my vision. When he checked my other eye – the one you've been working on – he found improvement there too. I can't believe it Ann, I've only had two healing sessions and both eyes are getting better."

I was astounded to find that her damaged left eye had responded to the healing, especially when I had not concentrated in this area. Neither did I expect a result this quickly. Although I wanted her to continue with the healing for the full six weeks, she only came for one further session. Despite this, her eyes continued to improve without my help, and she no longer needed to wear glasses to drive.

This was certainly a success story, almost a miracle judging by the speed at which healing took place, but I knew I could not take credit for it as I was used solely to pass the energy from spirit to Lee. Of course, not all healing produces these results. I believe that everyone has to fulfil his destiny, and some people have to do this while suffering terrible pain. I am aware though, that each person will receive some form of healing; if not physically, then certainly on an emotional, mental or spiritual level. There will always be sceptics who say it's all in the mind and that the healing has a placebo effect. Of course, a positive attitude will often help the body to heal more rapidly, but if we were all able to use the mind alone, we would not need a medical profession or any other form of alternative medicine.

Healing has been given to animals with wonderful results. Animals cannot analyse, and they often respond far quicker to healing than humans. Both Peter and I have given successful healing to animals over the years, but occasionally we have had our failures as well. We once had a Siamese cat, which was pregnant with her first litter. She began her labour before time and the first kitten was stillborn. The vet had to perform a caesarean section to remove the remaining three kittens. After experiencing this, the mother refused any contact with her litter, and I had to feed them hourly through the night. Despite my efforts, they all died. I was still holding the last kitten when I witnessed her soul leaving her body.

From the top of her head poured a substance that resembled smoke. This gradually formed into the shape of the kitten, and it was connected to the top of her physical head by a smaller tendril. As I watched in awe, a large, cupped hand appeared and gently held the tiny spirit as the tendril broke away. Both the hand and spirit kitten slowly disappeared. Since then, I have seen other souls leave the body at the moment of death, and there has always been someone from spirit to meet them.

I am a member of Horizon, a research foundation scientifically run by doctors at Southampton Hospital. They are conducting a study into the "Near Death Experience (NDE)" to see whether the mind is separate from the brain, so that it can live on after death. At one time, medical scientists believed drugs caused the NDE, but they have since discovered that this is not the case. Thanks to progress in medical science, more patients are resuscitated from clinical death and are able to report their experiences, which in many cases are very similar. They often say that they pass through a tunnel and are met by members of their family or a radiant being. In exceptional cases, some of these patients even saw people they thought were still alive. Other patients reported seeing visions of relatives appearing at their bedside shortly before they died. They were seen focusing their attention on a point in space where they saw the apparition.

A friend of ours, who was dying of cancer, would break off our conversation to stare and point at something only visible to him. Although at times he looked puzzled, he often smiled and nodded at whomever it was he could see. If someone is terminally ill, it gives the dying person a chance to come to terms with what is going to happen to him. These people may not realise they are being spiritually prepared for passing, and although they are often in pain, spirits are drawing close, preparing them for their rebirth to a higher level. Not only does this help the mind of the dying person, but it also gives the living the opportunity to come to terms with their loved-one's illness, and to say goodbye.

Many deaths occur suddenly. When this happens, those left behind suffer terribly, but in some cases warning signals have been given beforehand.

*

"Would you give me a Tarot card reading?" asked my cousin, Pat. She lived in America and was on a visit to England where she was staying with my parents for a few days. Pat was pleased with her reading. She told me it answered some questions in her mind that she had not voiced. My parents and younger brother had booked a holiday in America for October that year, and in return Pat had invited them back to stay with her.

"Will you lay the cards for me now?" asked my mum.

After she shuffled, I set the cards out in a spread predicting the future. I noticed the Death card sitting in her "house" of relationships. I was not unduly concerned, as this card nearly always represented a complete change.

"I have the travel card here, also one showing that you're still going to America with Mark, but it looks as though dad is staying behind."

She laughed and joked, "There's no chance we'll be going without him, as he's the one holding the money."

"Well, it looks to me as though you'll have a big argument over something, because the cards around it are pretty negative. He definitely isn't going, although you and Mark will go."

Being fairly sceptical, my mother simply passed it off as a bit of fun.

A few weeks later, I was standing outside a church in Kingston market chatting to my dad, when a funeral cortege came to a halt outside the gates. After watching silently, my dad said absently, "I wonder who'll be the next one passing through those doors?" For a few moments he looked lost in thought before turning back to me.

"There's an old wives' tale, Annie, that if a picture falls off a wall there will be a death in the family."

"Are you telling me a painting has fallen off your wall?" I asked.

He nodded, "Hmmm, and there's no reason why it should have happened, as the cord was still in one piece."

"Come on dad. You've just said it's an old wives' tale - a load of rubbish - surely you don't believe it?"

His face told me something different.

Shortly after this, my father's back gave way while he was lifting something heavy, and his doctor ordered bed rest. My mother had to go out for a while, leaving him alone. She asked me if I would go to their house and keep him company for a while. When I arrived Dad looked very lonely, lying flat on his back and unable to move.

After lunch, I sat with him for some time, talking about the family. Suddenly he changed the subject and said, "I saw Jesus Christ this morning. He came and stood at the bottom of my bed."

This took me totally by surprise, and for a moment I didn't answer.

"What do you mean dad? Are you saying you actually saw someone from spirit standing in front of you?"

He nodded. "He looked at me, smiled and held out his hands. Then he slowly disappeared."

"And you thought he looked like Jesus?"

"He was dressed in white robes and had a long beard and moustache. I'm telling you Ann, he was as solid as you or I, and he was standing there in front of me."

Turning his head towards me, he asked, "What do you think it means?"

Feeling uneasy, I said, "It sounds like a guide to me – perhaps one who's come to give you healing. They often appear dressed in robes."

He accepted my answer but I could see he was still unsure, so we changed the subject. A little later, I left him to return home.

Some time after he recovered, the family was invited to dinner at my parents' house. We were talking about a thousand and one different topics, when my dad produced a very old, large, black Bible. I leaned over the back of his armchair as he read the inscription inside the front cover. My father was not religious and this was the first time I had seen this Bible, although I had heard about it before. I didn't know whether he believed in God or the afterlife, but he had asked me a lot of questions about my mediumship, so I knew he had an open mind on the subject.

Later that week, I had a short but vivid dream that my mother had phoned me in the early hours of the morning to say my father had suddenly died. Unable to get back to sleep, I went downstairs and made myself a hot drink. A feeling of dread swept through me and I began to pace nervously back and forth in the living room. I could not get the dream out of my head. Something bad was going to happen, and because I felt it was connected to my dad I was unwilling to ask spirit what it was. It was only a matter of days before I found out. My dad and younger brother were leaving for work, when my dad said he couldn't breathe properly. In the time it had taken Mark to look back at him, my father died. My mum rang for an ambulance and then phoned me. It had happened exactly as my dream had shown me.

Dad's funeral service was held in the same church in Kingston market where he had first told me about the painting falling off his wall. I don't know if he was the next one to go through the church doors, but as he died so quickly after telling me about the picture, he could have been.

Although his passing was sudden, all the warning signs were there, both for him and for me. I had not wanted to acknowledge any of it because I couldn't face the possibility of him dying. I was too close to the whole situation to see it clearly. Even if I had known he was going to die, what could I have done? In his subconscious mind, my father was being prepared for his death. I think he knew this, especially when he saw the spirit standing at the bottom of his bed. In my heart, I knew it too.

Several weeks after the funeral, Nicky and I had a short holiday in Malta to help us come to terms with his passing. One morning, we were sitting on the balcony outside our room, eating breakfast and making plans for the day. Out of the corner of my eye I saw movement, and so did Nicky. Together, we turned towards the room. Standing in the doorway was my dad. He was smiling at us and he looked as though he had decided to join us for breakfast. Nicky called out "granddad" and got to her feet just as he began to disappear. I believe he had come to reassure us that he was alive and well.

Some months later, my eldest daughter Karen went into hospital to have her first baby. During the pregnancy, we had often wished that my father were still with us to see his first great-grandchild. After Gemma was born, Nicky, Chris (Karen's husband) and I went to the hospital to see them both. After a while, Chris left us alone to go to the hospital shop. The three of us were looking at Gemma, when for a moment my father's face was superimposed over hers. We realised he was with his great-grandchild after all.

21
The Missing Boy

"I'm desperate Mrs. Caulfield. My son is missing and I'm hoping you can help me find him!"

Mary was struggling to hold back her tears. Taking her through to my psychic room, I asked her to sit down and try to unwind a little while I made her a cup of tea. When I came back, I could see she was more composed, although her eyes still looked haunted. Mary lived on our estate, but I was only on nodding acquaintance with her. I was aware she had a family, but I had not heard that any of her children were missing.

Mary offered me a pair of spectacles. "The lady who lives next door to me told me that I should bring something for you to hold. Will these do?" she asked.

Sitting down opposite her, I held the spectacles, closed my eyes and asked spirit to help me. "My guide is showing me a young boy of about eleven. This child is not in spirit. His hair is brown and straight. He is always getting into scrapes of one kind or another. I can see him with his shirt hanging out and the buttons undone; and with scuffed shoes. He's full of energy and he can't sit still for two minutes."

"That sounds like him. He'll never do as he's told."

Interrupting, I said, "He's been missing for at least two weeks."

"Yes."

"I now have a picture of a man. He's not in spirit, either. I would guess his age to be somewhere in his late teens, or early twenties. He is about five feet ten inches tall and very slim. His hair is dark brown and he is clean-shaven. His shoulders are rounded, almost hunched, and he is a smoker. The man I can see is Irish like you are, Mary. He is not your relative, but he has close contact with your family. Your son is with him."

"You've described a friend of the family. He was living with us for some time and Patrick followed him everywhere. But what is he doing with Patrick now?"

"Spirit is telling me that he left your home at the same time that Patrick disappeared."

"Yes he did. However, he would not harm Pat in any way. We've known him for a long time." Her voice was rising. "I'm sure he wouldn't hurt him."

"No, I feel you're right. Spirit is repeating the message that they are together. I am now being shown a small, stone cottage. It is isolated and there is nothing else around for miles. It's in Ireland. There are rifles and other equipment lying on an old wooden table inside this cottage. It belongs to the IRA."

"Oh my God!"

"This young man has recruited your son into the IRA."

Spirit followed with further details about the route they had taken and their arrival in Ireland. I felt strongly that Mary would not see Patrick again, but I did not pass this information to her.

"You've confirmed what the police told me," Mary said as I passed the spectacles back to her.

"You've been to the police? My guide didn't tell me that."

"Yes. They told me they think he is in Ireland with Paul and that there is a connection with the IRA. They won't tell me any more than that, but when I leave here, I'm going straight to the police station to give them this information."

Mary came back later that evening to tell me what the police had said. "They recorded everything you told me.

Most of what you saw fits in with their investigation, and they are concentrating on Northern Ireland. They have the identity of others involved, but they would not tell me anything else until they have completed the case.

"Thanks for all your help, Mrs. Caulfield. I feel better knowing you have confirmed what the police believe. It's not knowing that makes it so difficult."

"Call me Ann," I said, giving her a hug. "And, if you need me again, you know where I am."

After she left, I returned to my room and thought about her situation. Despite being aware of her feelings of desolation, I really could not begin to imagine what she was going through. To lose a child, whatever the circumstances, must be horrific. My heart went out to her. Mary did not call on me again and I felt that I should not intrude.

We moved house a few months later, but before we did, our mutual neighbour, Brenda, told me that Patrick was still missing.

22

About Psychometry

Peter and my two brothers, Mark and John, had just returned from a fishing trip to Ireland. As he unpacked his clothes, Pete turned to me and said, "I've brought something back with me that I'd like you to psychometrise when you have the chance."

Intrigued, I said, "I'll give it a try now, if you like."

Turning, he lifted a small bag out of the suitcase and followed me into our quiet room. I made myself comfortable and tuned in. Pete sat in an armchair opposite me with a notebook and pen at the ready. When I opened my eyes, he reached into the bag and drew out a very small piece of stone. It was white, flat and chalky. Taking it from him, I gently turned it over in my hands. Almost immediately, I could feel heat coming from it.

"This is hot and getting hotter as I speak," I said. I closed my eyes and a picture formed in my mind. "I can see a huge fireplace. I'm certain that's where the stone has come from."

"Go on," Pete said.

"I'm now standing in the centre of a room. It looks as if it had once been split into two rooms. I'm sure there was once a curtain going across the middle."

Opening my eyes, I looked at Pete but he simply nodded.

Closing them again, I said, "In the fireplace is a huge, black pot hanging from a metal arm that you can swing back and forth so that it can be put into and taken out of the fire.

The pot looks something like a cauldron. It is that kind of shape. There is another one standing on the floor by the fire. Both pots have been used for cooking."

"Carry on," Pete urged.

"The room is fairly bare. There is a little wooden stand with drawers in it propped against the outside wall. There is a tiny window close by and there are a few small flowers on the sill. Other flowers and grasses lie on the floor and I am sure that they are herbs. Standing on a shelf are glass bottles with some kind of rough powder in them. There is a pestle and mortar nearby, where herbs have been dried and ground up to be used for something significant."

"Yes; go on."

"The other part of the room has a bed and an old wooden chair standing next to it. Now I am back in the first part of the room again. There is a stable door and the top half is open. I have opened the door and I am walking outside into a small dusty yard. I am turning and looking back at a small, stone cottage. There are a few chickens running around and a large pig. This is strange. The pig has moved inside the cottage, and is looking out at me over the stable door."

"Yes. That's right. Go on, don't stop now."

"Okay, okay," I answered, taking my energy higher and looking in my mind again.

"I'm still outside in the yard. There isn't much out here, though. I cannot see any other buildings close by. There could be some; it is just that I cannot see them. Now I am standing in front of water. It looks like a lake, but it's small. It's not a river and it's definitely not the sea. I can only describe it as a small lake."

Opening my eyes, I looked at Pete for confirmation. He nodded again.

I took my energy higher – and then everything changed. "A spirit woman has come through. She is somewhere between the ages of fifty and sixty. There are only a few lines on her face and she has a thick head of hair. I am sure she looks younger than she is. Although she is going grey, there are still streaks of light colour running through her hair. Her piercing blue eyes are looking right through me. She gives me the impression of being very serious. Her black skirt finishes just above her ankles and her feet are bare. She is wearing a black bodice with a light coloured shawl over the top. The shawl crosses over in front and it tucks into the waistband of her skirt. She is very psychic. You can tell that just by looking at her. In fact, I am sure she was a witch – a white witch. It is her cottage. I can now see her inside. She's mixing up the herbs."

I could hear Pete scribbling away as fast as he could. "Just a sec, let me get all of this down," he said as I carried on speaking.

I waited for a few moments until he was ready. "She's gazing into something. It looks as if she is scrying. I cannot make out what it is she's looking into though. It's something shiny like glass, but it's not the conventional crystal ball."

As he turned the page Pete remarked, "I don't believe I'm hearing all of this.

"Do you want me to go on?"

"Definitely."

"The woman has gone and I can see a small bridge. In the middle of it is a man sitting on a horse. He is trying to make the animal move by digging in his heels, but the horse will not have it. The man is dressed in a long, black robe. It is made of some kind of rough material, a bit like the skirt the woman was wearing. I have the impression he is a priest. Whoops. The scene has suddenly changed back to the woman looking at the glass, and then back to the man on the horse. She is connected to him in some way. I am back in the cottage. Inside is a man. I was just about to describe him, but another man has taken his place. There are men, women and children coming in and out of the cottage all the time. The energy is dropping and I am getting tired now, love, so I will have to leave it. Just one more thing - the lake: I've been taken back to it again, so it appears to have some kind of importance."

Opening my eyes, I could see that he was still writing. I rubbed my neck and shoulders, and closed myself down whilst he finished his notes.

"Well, what do you think?" I asked.

"I can't believe how accurate you were. The woman was a famous witch called Biddy Early. Her cottage was just as you described, and this piece of stone came from her fireplace. After she died, the cottage almost became a ruin, but someone has rebuilt it exactly as it was when she lived there. The only original bits are the fireplace and the stable door. I had permission to take this from inside the fireplace where there were a few loose pieces. There were herbs because she was a healer like her mother before her," he said grinning, "and she always used a pestle and mortar to grind them up. The pig was very significant, because she was fattening it up and she asked some friends if they would kill it for her, but instead they stole it and sold it on."

"Some friends," I remarked.

"You saw a priest on horseback standing on a bridge. Well, a priest had gone to see her and accused her of doing the Devil's work, and because she was angry with him for this, she put a curse on him. When he arrived at the middle of the bridge the horse wouldn't go any further, and no matter how hard he tried, he could not get off. They were both stuck there until another man came over the bridge. Realising by now that he had been cursed, the priest asked the man to go to Biddy Early to see if she would remove the curse. It took some persuasion but she did so, and the priest and horse went on their way again."

"It sounds to me as if there's quite a lot of myth woven into this story," I said.

"There probably is, but you still picked up the details from the stone. You could see her staring into glass and you thought she was scrying. She was; but she used a blue glass bottle to concentrate on. Apparently, her bottle had been thrown into a small lake after she died, but although the lake was later dredged and other glass and rubbish was found, her bottle was never retrieved. I would have to check out one or two of the things that you said, though. The dresser, for example. I don't know about that. There were always people in and out of her cottage, and I know she was married several times. I've no idea what she looked like or how she dressed, but I've brought you a book on her life, so you can check this out for yourself."

"Where did you hear all of this?" I asked him.

"The people who rented the holiday house to us are distantly related to Biddy Early. They live near her cottage and they showed us around. They were the ones who said I could take this piece of stone."

As I waited for Pete to find the book, I thought about what I had just achieved. Although I had given psychometry before on a personal level, this was the first time I had made a true attempt at something outside that range. It had all seemed so easy. Perhaps that was because I had given myself over completely to everything that I felt and saw. I didn't try to make sense of what I was receiving because I knew that could cause a barrier. I felt pleased that I had accomplished so much. If I could do this with nothing more than a small piece of stone, there must be other people who could tap into history in this way. I realised that if developed properly, psychometry could enable a person to achieve so much that is good.

On a clairvoyant level, Biddy herself chose to contact me. I felt privileged. After all those years, she must have evolved to a higher spiritual level. She was so clear. I could recall the weave in her scarf and skirt. Just below her chin were lines on her neck that her scarf did not cover. She had blemishes on her face, and some strands of her hair stood up with static electricity. I was on a high; I knew it would be some time before the adrenaline stopped pumping. Finding the story so intriguing, I couldn't wait to read the book, and when I did, it confirmed the parts Pete did not know about.

I have found that many mediums suffer adversity in their early years, and Biddy Early was no exception. It is as though they need to experience difficulties to enable them to grow spiritually.

There are many psychics around who use psychometry very successfully. Sometimes the police call upon these people to help them solve a case. Two of the most gifted and well-known psychic detectives of the twentieth century came from Holland. These were Gerard Croiset and Peter Hurkos, and both of them had had early premonitions of their later psychic talents. It came as no surprise to me to hear that Gerard Croiset had a very turbulent childhood. His father deserted him and his mother abandoned him; then he lived in a succession of foster homes. This hardship had helped him to develop his latent psychic ability. In the 1930s, he quickly gained a reputation as a psychometrist who could see into the past and present, and from this, he developed his mediumship and predicted future events.

One example of his gift was the story of the disappearance of a four-year-old child in New York. The child had been missing for three days when the police approached him for help. Declining the offer of a flight to New York, he asked for a photograph of the child, a map of New York, and an item of her clothing. After holding these in the same way that I had held the stone, he described the building where the child lay dead. He gave detailed descriptions of the murderer and of the crime. Several hours after giving this, the child's body was found in the building that Croiset had described. The police arrested the murderer after the property owner identified him as the person who had rented the room.

Peter Hurkos' career began after an accident. He fell four stories from a building he was painting in The Hague, in Holland. He was unconscious when he went to hospital, where doctors diagnosed him with concussion and possible neurological damage. Four days' later he regained consciousness, but he had amnesia. When his wife came to visit him, he became agitated, crying out to her that their son was trapped in a burning room. Five days later, his son was actually in a burning room, but fortunately, someone rescued him. This incident opened up his brilliant psychic pathway, and he became renowned throughout Europe and the United States as a psychic detective. The police asked him to work on well-known cases such as The Boston Strangler, where he would simply run his fingers across the back of photographs and describe different aspects connected to them.

On one occasion, the police asked him to help with the murder of a young coal miner in the Dutch province of Limburg. Hurkos ran his fingers over the man's coat, before telling the police that the miner's stepfather had committed the shooting. He said the murder weapon was on the roof of the dead man's house. Police found the gun exactly where Hurkos said it would be, and the fingerprints that they took from it led to the conviction of the stepfather.

To be able to use a psychic gift in this way must be so fulfilling. In my early days, I often thought of trying this direction myself. However, my guides have told me that, although psychometry will play a part on my pathway, I would channel my abilities into mediumship.

23
Remote Viewing

Some mediums do not become aware of their abilities until later in their lives. This sometimes happens after a traumatic experience as it did with Peter Hurkos. For others, it often comes with a spiritual awakening, such as in the case of my friend Dorothy Chapman. This is what she told me.

"My father-in-law was very ill. It was our turn to visit him and to sit with him throughout the night. By this time, he was close to death, and the nurse told us to expect this to happen around 2.30am."

"Were you frightened, knowing he would probably die whilst you were with him?" I asked.

"No – and as it happened, I sat with him on my own because Charlie was tired and fell asleep.

"About 2am I became aware of how quiet it was, when suddenly there was a lot of shouting outside of the door. I remember thinking that if whoever was making all the noise did not stop, I would have to go out and tell them that someone was dying in here. I turned towards the door and realised I could see right through it!"

"But surely that must have frightened you a little bit?"

"No it didn't, because I was too busy watching three little boys who were standing there. All three boys had fair hair. As I watched, other people came running up to stand behind them. I then heard the most beautiful music, but after a few minutes the music and the people faded away."

"What happened next?"

"Charlie woke up and we both saw that his father had passed over."

"So they must have been the spirits who had come to meet your father-in-law as he died."

"That's right, although I didn't know that then, of course. What I had seen astounded me, so when we got home I told my mother-in-law, and she said I had seen a manifestation from spirit. She advised me to find out more about it, and she suggested that I went to Morden Spiritualist Church the following Sunday. At the meeting, the medium came to me, giving me correct details of what had happened. She then recommended that Charlie and I should sit in a good circle to develop our mediumship. This was our first experience of anything psychic, but it did not take long before we were well and truly involved.

"We've now been practicing mediums for thirty-one years, and we wouldn't have changed any of it."

It may have taken a few years before Dolly had her eyes opened, but unlike me, she experienced no hesitation about her pathway when it appeared to her.

All mediums are born with strong psychic abilities, which they can trace back through one of their parents. My gifts seem to have emanated from both parents. My maternal grandmother was psychic, and she passed her gifts on to my mother. My father was also psychic, but as his parents had adopted him at an early age, I could not discover anything about his natural parents. Both of my children have inherited their psychic abilities from me, and it appears they have passed these onto my grandchildren. My eldest daughter, Karen, began using her mediumship at an early age in a similar way to me. Nicky did not develop her gifts as such, but she often had premonitions, most of which came to her in her sleep.

*

It has been common knowledge for many years that both the USA and the USSR trained psychics for spying purposes, but there still is not much open information on these activities. Over the years, I have found the most down-to-earth, sceptical people are those who often have strong, mediumistic gifts. David Morehouse is no exception.

Morehouse was a highly decorated army officer in the United States. He dealt with practical matters, and as a soldier, he was the most unlikely person to believe in the psychic field. Like Peter Hurkos, David discovered his psychic ability through an accident; in his case, this was after a bullet had hit his helmet and knocked him out. The CIA then recruited David Morehouse as a psychic spy. Stargate was one of the most secret programs of espionage ever instigated by the CIA. The CIA trained him to be a "remote viewer", and he later exposed the scandalous facts about this program to the world. The army almost succeeded in destroying him and his family, but he came through it and went on to teach others the same techniques that he had used when working for Stargate.

The mind itself is a powerful tool, which, when properly trained, can produce fantastic results. In the early years of our mediumship, Pete and I formed a small group of mediums to experiment in remote viewing. Each week one of us would choose a destination to visit. The rest of us then sat separately in our own surroundings, attempting to "see" the journey that the other person was taking. The experiment and the person's journey occurred simultaneously, so it was not possible to pick up thoughts about what the person might see along the way beforehand. The traveller himself did not know in advance what he would encounter along he way. Despite being amateurs, at times the results were astonishing. One member visited an art gallery in London, and was "seen" walking up the steps to the building. Most of the group also received details of various paintings, the time on a clock at the café where he stopped for coffee, and various landmarks he encountered on his way home. When it was my turn, I chose to visit a zoo, but only one or two saw anything that connected to that trip.

We were in the early stages of experimentation, so it was not always successful. We had to consider many things and the conditions had to be right. For example, if the remote viewers' environment was noisy, it was difficult to concentrate. The weather made a difference. A clear, sunny day seemed to produce better clairvoyance. Obviously, anyone feeling below par would have had difficulty tuning in. We would probably have had better results if we had been able to do this under the kind of controlled conditions in which David Morehouse had worked.

We continued to experiment with remote viewing for several months before the group broke up, but even in this short time, we discovered just what the mind could achieve. "Psycho-kinesis" is the name for power of mind over matter, and people have proved on many occasions that it works. For years, mediums in Russia have been photographed moving objects with their minds under controlled scientific conditions. Although I have not achieved this, on one occasion, Pete was reading his newspaper when, for want of nothing better to do, I attempted to make his face itch. Concentrating hard, over and again, I tried to make his nose itch so that he would have to scratch it. To my surprise, it only took a few moments before he began to rub his nose. Next, I focused on his ear; and sure enough, he began to scratch it. This made me laugh, so he stopped reading and asked me what was so funny.

"I've been trying to see if I could make your nose and ear itch and both times you've scratched yourself."

"Hmm," he grunted, picking up the paper again and ignoring me.

Once more, I centred my energy - this time to both his ears. After a few moments, I noticed that he was gripping the paper tightly and that his knuckles were white. I kept up the concentration, until he suddenly threw his paper across the floor and scratched furiously at his ears. I will not repeat the names that he called me! Of course, this was only a small example of what the mind can do, but it would not be hard to imagine what one could produce under tightly controlled conditions for a spying program.

Healing, psychometry and dowsing (the ability to feel the presence of underground water or minerals) are widely reported. It is clear that the mere functioning of the physical brain cannot explain these phenomena. I have experimented with Zenner cards, each of which carries a basic drawing. The illustrations might be of a house, a flower, a number and so on. The sender shuffles the cards and sits opposite the receiver. The sender takes a card, studies it, and then tries to "send" a mental picture of the illustration to the receiver. The receiver then says what he can see in his mind, or he tries to draw it. When the subject has used all the cards, the tester calculates the score. Many, many times we have succeeded in getting at least 50 per cent of them right.

Telepathy is one faculty that almost everyone is aware of, because most people experience this at some point in their lives. This so-called "sixth sense" that is used when a person is aware of someone else's thoughts is so very common - and yet scientists say that this power cannot exist, because it has no physical basis. For similar reasons, science also states that precognition (viewing the future) cannot exist; yet this is something I have been able to do since childhood. I hear lately that scientists experimenting with Quantum Physics have discovered behaviour of some minute particles that can only be explained by travelling through time! Who knows, perhaps their opinions may yet become more realistic than they have been so far.

It is doubtful that scientists will ever fully understand how the psychic faculty works, but at least it is gratifying to know that many of them now accept they do not have all the answers. It is important to keep an open mind, but it is not necessary to know how it works – only that it does.

24
Was it Possession?

Three years after my father died, we moved from Surrey to Woodgreen, a small village in the heart of the New Forest, not far from the south coast of England. We bought a small bungalow with a large garden, and the forest surrounded the property on two sides. The village is picturesque, with horses, cattle and pigs roaming freely, and is famous for its outstanding natural beauty. There was a village hall, a butcher, post office and grocery store and, of course, a pub. There were no streetlights, so venturing out after dark meant taking a flashlight. When we were living in the busy area of Kingston in Surrey, I didn't even know where the flashlight was kept!

As we were new to the area, but still wanted to work on a psychic level, we decided to become members of the Spiritualist Church in the nearby town of Bournemouth. The people at the Church invited us to become healers and they also asked me to teach development classes. Pete still had to earn a living in the normal way – and in addition - we were both giving healing and teaching at home. Within a short space of time, the work snowed us under. Something had to go, and I decided it was to be my platform work.

Meanwhile, people in the village gradually became aware of my profession. Some people who had previously spoken to us decided to avoid me, while others called on me for readings. I ignored the hostile attitude I received from a few villagers, and soon settled down to country life. It did not take long for us to find out that living in a small village was very different to living in a large town.

Owing to the lack of street lamps, I would look out of my window to see a line of bobbing lights when members of my class followed each other up the path. At other times, my class would be disrupted while we all dived into the garden to chase out the horses that had learned to roll across the cattle grid or the cows that had jumped over the gate. This meant that I had to learn to relax some of the discipline that Ivy had imbued in me.

I sometimes gave my students information about other psychic pathways, but I always impressed on them the importance of protecting themselves on a psychic level. On one occasion, I had been discussing the different methods used for scrying.

"One way of developing clairvoyance is by using a bowl filled with ink," I told them. "The scryer should sit for a few minutes, quietly gazing at the surface of the ink, where a picture will eventually form. This will not happen immediately, so the scryer should practice doing this on several occasions." I then went into further detail as to how this should be done, finishing with a warning. "As you're developing your clairvoyance in class, I don't want any of you to try scrying at home on your own. Sitting by yourself at this stage of your development can leave you open to things entering your aura from the lower astral plane."

There is always one, isn't there? In this case, it was a student named Carol who thought otherwise.

Carol was a quiet woman who did not push herself forward in the class. She frequently ran her own abilities down, saying that everyone else was so much better than she was. One day, she appeared to be more confident, joining in with the others when I asked if anyone had received clairvoyance. Then she let slip that a man from spirit was telling her what to do. When questioned about her spirit friend, she told us she had been scrying when he first made contact with her. Further probing revealed that she had been sitting for a long time while staring into a bowl of black ink. Apparently, when she finally packed it away, she collapsed. The students sat in stunned silence at her tale of stupidity.

While Carol was telling us her story, I looked into her aura, but I couldn't see anything or anyone with her. However, I knew very well how something unpleasant could hide itself.

"Stay behind after the class Carol," I said, "and we'll have a chat, but for now we should get on with the rest of the lesson." As soon as the class finished, people surrounded me to ask questions about one thing or another – but Carol had disappeared.

I did not want to wait until the next session before contacting her. If what she said was true, it was important to find out more about the "spirit" man whom she had told us about, so the following morning I phoned her.

"Can you tell me how long you were scrying for?"

She was wary. "Well, I must confess, I scryed for longer than I should have done."

"How long was that? An hour or two?"

She was reluctant to answer, but I was shocked when she finally said, "No. It was on and off all day and most of the evening."

"Oh, Carol, what did I tell you? You must only scry for a few minutes at a time, and definitely not on your own."

"I know, I know. It's my own fault. I just wanted to be able to see something."

"And did you?"

"No. But I began to feel uncomfortable."

"In what way?"

"I felt there was someone with me," she responded.

"Did you decide to stop at this point?"

"No, because I thought I had a guide drawing close to me."

"Guides wouldn't make you feel uncomfortable, Carol. So how are you feeling now?"

"Not too bad."

She sounded cagey.

"So, you're not feeling too good either?" I asked.

She hesitated…

"Come on Carol. What's happened?"

"I can hear someone swearing at me all the time," was her surprising answer.

"What? Is this inside your head or externally?"

"Inside," she answered quietly.

"Look, under no circumstances are you to do anything else on a psychic level. Whenever you hear the voice; ignore it, and close down your centres and bring the light through. This is important Carol, because if this doesn't work, I will have to find someone who can help you to get rid of whatever it is you have attracted to yourself.

"I'll ring you tomorrow to see how you are, but you must promise me until then that you'll leave your psychic side alone except to close and cleanse."

"What should I do about the class next week?" she asked.

"I'm sorry Carol, but you'll have to stay away until this is sorted out."

"Why?" Carol was clearly puzzled by my response.

"If something has attached itself to you, it will draw energy from the students and become stronger, and then it will become more difficult to exorcise. There could be a danger to the others as well as you. Just do as I ask for a short while and we'll go on from there."

"Oh all right," she said, cutting the call without saying goodbye.

I spoke to her the following day, and she told me that the voice was swearing violently and more frequently, despite her attempts at closing down her chakras.

"In that case I'll speak to someone who can help you," I promised.

I do not specialise in exorcism, but there are people who work exclusively in this area. One of the dangers of exorcism is that if it the exorcist does not perform it correctly, the unwanted entity can leave one person and climb into the aura of another person. I tried to reassure Carol before telling her that I would ring back as soon as I had been in touch with someone who could help her. I contacted an exorcist and he explained that he worked with a team of two people. He said that it was definitely possible that she had drawn an unwanted spirit to her, despite the fact that this was a rare occurrence. The exorcist had a warning for me though. He told me that sometimes a person will say these things just for attention, so he would need to assess the situation to see whether the possession was genuine or not.

I phoned Carol but there was no answer, so I assumed she had gone out. During the day, I rang her intermittently but was still unable to reach her. Over the following two days, I continued to telephone to no avail. In the end, I contacted another student in my class to see if she had heard anything. The student said, "I saw her in the town shopping, but we didn't speak. She looked perfectly okay to me, but I'll pop round to her and see if I can find out what's going on."

There was no sign of Carol at the next class. At first, I thought she had stayed away because I had asked her too. However, her friend said that when she spoke to Carol, she told her she was so upset because I would not let her back into the class. Indeed, she had ignored the ringing phone because she had guessed that I was calling her. She fumed so much over this supposed slight that she had decided to speak to a Catholic priest. After telling him the story, the priest had told her I was evil and that all my students and myself were consorting with the Devil. She added that the priest had exorcised the "evil spirit" from Carol with only one touch of his hand!

We didn't hear from Carol again. My feeling is that the so-called evil spirit had been a figment of her imagination. Carol was desperate for others to consider her a good psychic, and she was angry at her lack of talent, so this had been her way of getting attention. If she had truly been possessed, it would have taken far more than a touch to exorcise it from her.

25

A Medium's Notebook

Life is like a raindrop on a lotus leaf.
George Harrison

My teaching grew and I became so busy that I had to turn down applicants because there was not enough room for them. Not every student completed the course, but those who did, discovered that their lives were profoundly changed. Some of the students did not wish to use their psychic abilities in the same way as I did, as not everyone held my beliefs. Some of them were Spiritualists, but others followed different religions or were still searching for their own spiritual pathway. The one thing they had in common was a spiritual and psychic gift, which, once developed, enabled them to help others. They became healers, teachers, platform mediums, psychometrists or psychologists. Each of them had been given a spiritual awakening at some point, which they needed to fulfil. Most of the students became close friends, both in and outside the classes, with several becoming romantically involved with each other.

Some people found it difficult to come to us for healing, so we would go to visit them; and this was especially so when an animal was in need of our help. On one occasion, a young woman in the village approached Pete to ask for healing on her sick horse. He arrived at the paddock to find a nervous mare with a badly swollen knee. Looking into her eyes, he spoke quietly, trying to reassure the animal and telling her that he meant no harm. After a few minutes, the mare became calmer and eventually stood patiently whilst Pete gently placed his hands around her leg. Afterwards, she nuzzled his hand as if to say she understood what he was doing. By the following week, the swelling had reduced and the mare was walking better. After only a few sessions, her knee was back to normal and her owner was riding her again.

Most patients came to us as a last resort after conventional treatment had failed. Sometimes it would take only one or two sessions, but for the majority of people, it would take several weeks to bring about any change. While we were healing at Bournemouth Church, Pete treated a patient who suffered from emphysema. The poor man could hardly walk, and he spoke with difficulty because he couldn't get his breath. He had previously been a heavy smoker, although by the time he came to Pete he had stopped this habit. Pete gave him healing for six months and during that time his condition improved to the extent that he could climb stairs without becoming breathless. The healing did not cure the condition but it did prevent it getting worse, and it eased most of his symptoms.

On many occasions, we discovered that the underlying cause of symptoms was emotional, and once we had tackled this, the physical symptoms quickly disappeared. Naturally, there were also many people with far more serious conditions. One woman had angina, nervous problems, dizziness and general aches and pains. As I placed my hands on her, I was clairvoyantly shown, a picture of her heart and lungs. The picture altered to a close-up view of a heart valve. My spirit doctor told me that this valve was sluggish so he would concentrate mainly in this area. When she arrived the following week, I asked her how she was feeling.

"I've been remarkably well until yesterday. Since then I've felt extremely tired," she answered.

"Well, it looks as though something is beginning to work, so hopefully there will be more improvement this week."

Again, I was shown a close up of her heart and the sluggish valve, but to a non-medical person like me, it all looked pretty much the same.

"Please suggest to the patient that she removes vitamins B2 and B6, plus calcium from her diet," said the authoritative voice of my spirit doctor.

On arriving for her third appointment, she appeared to have more energy and stood straighter, without holding on to the chair. "I've been feeling much better this week, and I haven't had any dizziness either. The last two days I've felt tired, but I can hardly complain about that," she said as she made herself comfortable on the seat.

This time when I was shown inside her body, I had the impression that her heart was pumping a little better, and my spirit doctor confirmed this. Before her next visit, she had an appointment at the hospital for heart tests. Her consultant was pleased to find there was more improvement than he had expected. When I next saw the lady, she had a heavy cold and a sore throat and she was feeling generally under the weather.

"I suggest that she drinks barley water with cloves to soothe her throat and to help her cold," said my doctor, "and you can tell her that her angina is improving."

She was a different woman when she next arrived for healing.

"I can't begin to tell you how well I'm feeling. I haven't had as many pains in my chest and my circulation has improved. You didn't know that I have arthritis in my back, but I've been completely pain-free this week."

After four months of healing, it was time to say goodbye. She left my house feeling as though her life had been given back.

However, there were always some who simply did not respond to healing, and we could only suggest they saw someone else who worked with a different spirit doctor. After all, on our earth-plane they would be referred to different specialists, and it seems to be the same in the spirit world. When we could not help people with contact healing, we always added them to our absent healing list. Sometimes they would let us know of their progress, but more often than not, we wouldn't hear from them again, and the same would apply to readings. It was inevitable that I would sometimes come out with something during a reading that the client could not accept, and in this case I would always tell them to hold onto the information, as it would often show itself at a later date.

Two young women came to see me. The first lady was pleased with her reading, but her friend could not agree to anything that I gave her.

"You've recently separated from your husband and need guidance in which direction you should go."

"No, I haven't", she said looking puzzled.

"Oh, I'm sorry. I've obviously got that wrong."

Turning again to spirit, I asked for further information.

Once more I was told that she and her husband had just separated.

"The same message is being repeated," I told her, thinking that perhaps she was trying to catch me out.

"You're totally wrong," she said with some conviction.

Making sure I had made a proper link with her, I took my energy higher. "My guide is telling me that you're looking for somewhere else to live. He's now taking me inside a building that looks like a block of apartments. You have stopped outside a door and unlocked it, and now you are walking through each of the rooms, opening cupboards and examining other features. You seem to be pleased and satisfied with what you can see." I then went on to describe the layout of the rooms, including the colour scheme. "I'm now seeing a picture of you after you have moved in. There is a young boy with you. I believe he is your son. You are surrounded by cardboard boxes which you are unpacking. But there is no sign of your husband."

"Well yes, I have a son, but the rest of the message doesn't make any sense. I have no intention of moving, so the apartment doesn't mean a thing. We're very happy where we are."

"Just a moment," I interrupted, 'I'm being shown a woman who is on the earth plane. I will give you a description to see if you recognise her. If you don't, there'll be no point in continuing with this reading."

After describing the woman, my sitter shook her head. "I honestly don't know what on earth you are talking about."

"In that case, I won't take this any further. I'm really sorry but I can only give you what I'm being shown."

As they walked out the door, they looked at each other and I saw her friend raise her eyebrows and pull a face.

Well, I won't be seeing those two again, I thought as I watched them walk down the path, but to my astonishment, I later received a telephone call from the second sitter asking for another appointment. When she arrived, she simply asked me to try once more to see if I could get anything different from the last time. The message was the same.

She admitted that after leaving my home, they were laughing about me and saying what a load of old rubbish I was, but that very same evening, she had quite a nasty shock. Her husband told her he had been having an affair and that he was leaving her. As her divorce progressed, she could not afford to stay in the house, and had looked for an apartment to move into with her son. She had found one matching the description I had given her, and they were due to move within the next two weeks. The woman I had described in my clairvoyance fitted her husband's girlfriend.

Spirit has told me that time, as we know it, does not exist on the spiritual planes, and therefore they can only give approximate dates. With this reading, I felt that spirit couldn't have been much closer in its timing. I believe that our path of fate is already mapped out for us before we are born into this world, and this is often confirmed through the readings I give. Our ultimate destination has already been agreed, but our choice of pathway on arriving here is down to us. If this were not so, I could not give details of future events.

Mrs. Robinson came to me for a reading, and my guide told her something she did not want to hear.

"Your son is working abroad," I said.

"Yes," replied Mrs. Robinson.

"He's unhappy in his marriage and contemplating a divorce."

Shaking her head she answered, "No that's not true."

I asked for further information and my guide repeated it.

I told her, "Your son will be in touch with you soon. He wants a divorce, but needs to make sure he's doing the right thing before telling you."

She looked at me with disbelief but said, "Okay. I'll have to wait and see if he tells me."

"My guide says that he knows you find this hard to accept, but it really is for the best. Your son and daughter-in-law have been miserable for a long time."

"If that's the case, they've hidden it well, because they've always seemed perfectly all right to me."

Continuing, I said, "I'm being shown a picture of a young woman. She isn't in spirit, but I'll describe her to see if you recognise her."

She was shaking her head before I had finished. "No, I don't know who she is."

"I've been given the name, Jill, and this is the woman your son will meet at a later date, and whom he'll eventually marry."

Despite being sceptical of this information, she wrote it down, dated it, and said she would keep it safe to see what would happen. About two years later, she phoned for another appointment. "Is it okay to bring a friend with me?" she asked.

"Yes, of course you can," I answered.

When they arrived, I thought her friend looked familiar. "I know your face. Have you been to see me before?" I asked.

"No. This is my first time." Then the two women looked at each other and grinned.

After bringing in coffee, I studied her face again. "Are you sure we haven't met? You look so familiar to me."

"No. I've never seen you before, but I do believe you know of me." Now I was intrigued.

"I think it's time to tell her, don't you," Mrs. Robinson said, laughing.

"You've met Jill, but not in the conventional sense. This is the "Jill" you told me my son would meet."

Still perplexed I asked her to explain. She then reminded me about her last reading. "At the time I was totally sceptical, but I wrote the information down and kept it and am so glad that I did. Look, I've brought it with me to show you. The description is perfect."

Taking the piece of notepaper from her, I saw it was dated from two years before. The paper smelt a little musty, and there were holes in some of the creases where it had been folded and unfolded so many times. The description of "Jill" was the same person sitting in front of me, even down to the colour of her eyes. No wonder I thought I recognised her. This surely was proof that our destiny is already laid out before us. When she first came to see me, Mrs. Robinson had no idea about her son's unhappiness. At that time, he was still contemplating a divorce and "Jill" was way off in his future.

Another example of future events relates to a young woman named Alison. Her great-grandfather came through from spirit, and although she had never met him, her mother recognised his description. During the reading, evidence was given about many events connected with his life, and with what was happening around Alison.

"You have some difficulty with your right ankle, and it will need medical attention as time goes on," I told her.

"I haven't had any problems at all," said Alison.

"Good, I'm pleased to hear it, but just be aware that if this happens, you should get it looked at. Your great-grandfather says you're allergic to bananas, dairy products and red wine."

"No, I'm not. I've never had a problem with any of them."

"Well, this is all on the cassette, so whatever you do, don't throw it away. Keep it safe and play it every once in a while. Often things don't show themselves until a later date." I went on. "He's now telling me that if you marry the man you're involved with, your marriage will not last a year."

"We've been together for seven years, so I can't see that happening if we get married."

Her great-grandfather then showed me a picture of a man living on the earth plane. He told me she would marry this person. I described him to her; and I also described where they would live after they were married. "He hasn't come into your life yet. When you meet him he will be living in an apartment within a three-story building that will be located down a narrow alleyway. The entrance lobby has a long flight of stairs with a window at the top."

Although Alison could not accept this message, other information proved to be correct, so she did as I asked and held on to the tape recording. She kept in contact with me over the following months and years to tell me of her progress. Within six months of her first reading, she was diagnosed with rheumatoid arthritis, and this had started its appearance in her right ankle. A year after the reading, she discovered she was allergic to the foods and drink her great-grandfather had told her about. If she ingested these, within minutes her joints would swell. She ignored her great-grandfather's advice and went on to marry her current boyfriend, but the marriage was over within a year.

Five years later, she met and married the man her great-grandfather had shown me. His apartment was as shown to me, in the three-story building, down the narrow alleyway I had described. Once again, this proves that our fate is set in advance of our birth.

On another occasion, Alison asked me for a postal reading. On receiving the letter, I held it between my hands and sent energy towards it, tapping into Alison's aura from her energy that had become impregnated into the notepaper. This time her grandfather drew close to me, accompanied by another relative. I gave their descriptions and further evidential information about their lives. Alison had asked in her letter if she would ever become pregnant. She didn't think she could, because of her illness and the medication she was on. Spirit showed me a picture of her holding a baby boy aged about six months. They told me she would become pregnant within the next three to four years.

Several years later, she became the mother of a beautiful baby boy.

A young woman from a neighbouring village had a consultation with me. She was told that she would become a well-known artist. Laughing at this, she thought it would be very unlikely, as she didn't even possess a paintbrush. Two years later she exhibited her art at the Royal Academy in London!

Although spirits often predict the future, the main emphasis of mediumship is to prove survival of death. As with Alison's readings, it is always important to see if deceased relatives or friends will make contact with the sitter. However, often someone will come through, of whom the sitter has no knowledge, and the sitter must then check out the message. This proves that the information is not picked up from the sitter but from some outside influence. For instance, I have told many women about miscarriages or abortions they have had. Naturally enough, some of these incidents have been kept secret for one reason or another. When I pass information on that these babies have continued to grow in spirit, they are often surprised or shocked to learn about it. The babies or children come through with a relative or guardian so that messages can be given concerning their passing. I'm told they choose their way of dying before they are born. Everything we do in this physical life is a lesson to be learnt, either for our own sake or for someone else's.

I have had many spirits come through who have died in traumatic circumstances. Without exception, each one has told me they did not feel any pain on passing over.

A husband and wife came to see me. I tuned in and a young girl quickly showed herself. She told me she had died in an accident. "That's my mum and dad," she said.

"I have a young girl here with me, and she's saying you are her parents."

They both nodded, and the woman said, "Yes."

Turning back to the child, I asked her how old she was when she died.

"I was ten. I died in a car crash, but I didn't feel any pain. Well, not much, just a quick pain in my left arm but nothing after that."

After relaying this message, her mother replied, "It was her left arm and shoulder that were crushed during the accident."

The child continued. "The crash was eighteen months ago, but since then I've been to see my sister Lisa lots of times, so we can talk to each other. I'm in the house a lot and my mum speaks to me in her dreams."

"That is so true!" her mother exclaimed, "and her sister's name is Lisa."

"My dad is very bitter about the accident. Please tell him no one is to blame for what happened."

Her father confirmed he was still feeling this way. As he spoke to me, their daughter moved between them, placing her arms around their shoulders before leaning over to kiss them. She continued to give me evidential details about her father's work and other matters within the family. This little girl showed her parents how happy she was in spirit. She wasn't in pain and she wanted them to stop grieving and move on in their lives. Naturally, this is easier said than done. It must have been so difficult for them. None of us expect our children to die before we do.

I have often felt pain from spirit myself, although only to a small degree. I'm sure this is conveyed to make me aware of what the person suffered, and then enable me to express it in a way that can be understood. One man who had committed suicide drew a little too close for comfort.

On tuning in, I felt the sensation of a tight rope around my neck. Finding myself short of breath, I had to ask the spirit to stand back, whilst I cleansed myself of the sensation. The dead person had hung himself, so I asked him to show me this, rather than make me feel it. There are some people who believe that suicides go to a spiritual hell, but I have found this to be untrue. Firstly, there is no such place as hell. When we die, each of us must account for our actions, and we are all given the opportunity to come into the light and to progress, no matter what we have done. If someone is so unhappy that they feel the only way out of their misery is to kill themselves, they are considered to be psychologically ill, so they will not be condemned for being unable to cope. They will be given an opportunity of reincarnating so that they can continue the lessons that were terminated in the foreshortened life.

It is not always easy for spirit to convey pictures or information to a medium. It is rather like using a telephone in an area where there is poor reception. Sometimes the line is clearer than at other times. Much also depends on the spirits making contact, especially if it is their first time working with a medium.

I find it a great deal easier to give a reading if the sitter sits quietly and answers with a simple "yes" or "no" or "I don't understand." This way, I can use the sitter's energy and voice without being influenced by questions or information that I have not asked for. A sitter always has questions, but I try to leave these for the end of the reading. One small example of this was when another medium came to see me. Her guide, a huge Native American Indian, quickly showed himself. After describing him, I told her of the tremendous power he radiated.

"Yes, that's a good description, and it certainly sounds like him. Can you give me his name?"

Laughing I answered, "You of all people should know better than to ask me that. My head will be full of names now. I'll carry on with the reading, and hopefully he'll find a way of dropping it in."

Halfway through the reading I saw a teddy bear. When pressed as to why he had given it to me, he laughed and told me to repeat it to her. "For some unknown reason he's just shown me a teddy bear, but there isn't any information on this. Does it mean anything to you?"

After thinking for a few moments, she shook her head. "No, I can't place that."

I asked her guide for further information, and he showed me a huge, naked foot. "Now this is really daft, but I have to give it to you. He's just shown me a large, naked foot," I said.

She burst out laughing. "He's just told you his name. It's Bare Foot! I knew he'd find a way of getting it across."

Another young lady wanted her father to confirm the nickname that he had given her as a child.

"I've got a hundred and one names going through my head which I know are coming from my own mind, so hopefully he'll find a way of telling me during the reading." Sure enough, half way through, he gave me information that didn't make sense to me, but certainly did to her. "He's showing me a picture of a pig. He won't tell me why, but keeps repeating "pork chop, pork chop." He says I have to give it to you exactly as I'm seeing and hearing it."

"Oh heavens, Ann, that's all the proof I need. His nickname for me was "pork chop" until I was about ten years old."

There is no doubt in my mind, that spirits will go to any length to prove they are still alive, and that death is only a transition in an ever-evolving cycle.

26

In Sickness and in Health

Despite the fact that I had more than enough psychic work at home, I would sometimes spend a weekend away with friends at a psychic show. A promoter would book a venue and fill it with people selling crystals, jewellery, books and other items related to the psychic scene. This is an arduous way of giving readings, because the noise is horrendous and total concentration is required to block it out.

People have asked me why I did it. The answer is simple. There are many people who, for various reasons, will not make direct contact with a medium. However, under the guise of "having a bit of fun" at a psychic fair, spirit would still guide them to me. Men in particular were often reluctant to allow others to think that they needed help; some would sprawl back in the chair, grinning and giving the impression that it was all one big joke. These were usually the easiest to work with, and more often than not, they would ask for a card so they could contact me at home later.

Of course, as in any business, there will always be charlatans, and the psychic field has its fair share of these. Unfortunately, these frauds have no compassion for the emotional damage they can cause, as their main objective is the money they make from the misery of others. My advice to anyone seeking a reading with a reputable medium is to contact a Spiritualist Church and ask for a recommendation. Failing that, they can contact The Spiritualist Association of Great Britain, or The College of Psychic Studies in London. If someone is visiting a psychic show, they should always walk around the venue first, looking at each psychic, and then follow their feelings as to which one they should visit.

A friend may give a glowing account of a medium who she consulted, but unless you feel the need to see the medium yourself, do not be persuaded to pay him a visit. It is essential that you only have a reading because you really want one, otherwise you could be disappointed.

On one occasion, we went to a psychic fair in Glastonbury with Dolly and Charlie. As we pulled into the car park, we saw a woman and a man standing outside the entrance. She was short and plump, dressed entirely in black and was holding a long walking stick. The man was tall and thin, and wore an ordinary shirt and jeans. A large group of people surrounded the couple, so we had some difficulty getting by them in order to enter the building. We found our seats and looked with interest around the hall; on the opposite side to us were several vacant tables, but everywhere else, people were busily setting up their stands. Pete was reading the program, and pointed out that "Merlin and Morgana" were also booked to appear.

There was a sudden commotion at the door, and the couple we had seen outside walked in, with the same group of people trailing along behind. The woman walked to the centre of the floor and banged her walking stick several times to get everyone's attention. The crowd followed and formed a large circle around her. They began chanting. As they chanted, they did a weird sort of shuffle clockwise: then they turned and repeated the steps. They joined hands and ran towards her, shouting, "She's a witch, she's a witch, she's a witch, witch, witch!" Each time they did this, she stamped the floor again and again with her stick. They were desperately serious, but everyone else in the room doubled up laughing.

After a few minutes, they all huddled together whispering, before turning and walking out of the door. Soon they were back, carrying several computers between them. They plugged these in to use for their ready-made psychic readings, before placing a sign on the wall stating "Merlin and Morgana". Somehow, the archaic images of witches and warlocks did not have quite the same ring with a computer printout.

Despite working at a show, in a church or giving a lecture, the base for my psychic work was my house. Spirit had told me many years before that I must work from home and not anywhere else. However, I had now reached a point where my house was being used to the exclusion of anything other than my work, and we felt we should find premises elsewhere. By doing this, we might find it easier to "switch off" from the psychic field on returning home. Eventually we found a place in Ringwood, and set it up as a Foundation for Psychic Studies. Although we gave readings, healing and other events, the main emphasis was on teaching. It was impossible to do everything between us, and so my daughter Karen helped us with some of the teaching and workshops. A friend of ours, Peter Shenton, who is a superb teaching medium, also offered to hold some of the classes for us. We began to build the Foundation slowly, but I now found myself spending nearly every day and several evenings a week away from home.

I knew it would not be easy and that it could take several years to really become established, so when I began to feel the familiar niggles of premonition, I tried to ignore them. Every now and again though, I would think back to what spirit told me years before - i.e. that I should not take my psychic work elsewhere. Trying not to dwell on this, I continued with the Foundation. Although I was becoming increasingly tired, I convinced myself it would all be worth it in the end. The tiredness began to take its toll and I became stressed. Once again, I found myself having involuntary OBEs.

One night, after a particularly weary day, I came out of my body to find myself facing downward and wedged between the springs and stuffing of my mattress. I began to panic when I found I couldn't move, as I was not yet free of the paralysing stage. In my fright, I shot upwards like an elastic band. When my astral body returned to the physical, I woke to find myself with my head buried in my pillow.

On another occasion, I had travelled through my bedroom ceiling and up into the loft. I passed through spider webs and dust, and was about to pass through the roof, when I finally controlled my return to my physical body. These OBEs were unwanted symptoms of what was to follow.

One Friday morning, I awoke with the impression of something in my right eye. Rubbing it didn't make any difference, and on peering into the mirror, I couldn't see anything. Despite this, I was still aware of a small, black, oblong shape in my vision. After arriving at the Foundation, I asked Karen if she could see a speck of black in my eye, such as mascara, but she could not find anything either. All over the weekend this black oblong persisted. It was beginning to worry me, so on Monday morning I made an appointment with the optician.

He examined my eye thoroughly without making any comment before sitting in front of me with his hands clasped together. "I want you to go to Bournemouth Eye Hospital so they can examine it with better equipment than I have here," he told me.

"Why? What's wrong?"

"It's not clear enough for me to give you a diagnosis," he answered.

"But you must have some idea otherwise you wouldn't send me to hospital."

"I think you should leave this to the experts. It's important that you go as soon as you leave here, and make sure you have someone who can go with you," he said.

It was obvious I was not going to get anything more from him, yet his concern made me realise that I might have a serious problem. I made my way home to where Pete was waiting for me, and within minutes, we were on our way. When we arrived, we found the building packed, and as I didn't have an appointment, it was several hours before I saw anyone.

"Have you had any headaches?" the consultant asked me as he peered into my eye with a large metal and glass object.

"No."

He transferred the object to my left eye, and said "Hmm" a couple of times, before setting it down. "You've had what is known as an optical occlusion," he said.

"What does that mean?" I asked.

"You've had a small stroke. A blood vessel has burst at the back of your right eye. You have been very lucky, because you could have lost your sight. I'm surprised that you've not had any other symptoms."

I looked at him in amazement. "What on earth has caused that?"

"That's for us to find out. We'll transfer you to Salisbury hospital for a few tests, but until then, it's important that you take it easy."

"What do you mean by taking it easy? I have my own business and there isn't anyone else who can run it for me."

"If you don't rest, you may have another stroke, which could be bigger and far more damaging than this one."

Feeling stunned, I walked outside to where Pete was waiting. One look at my face told him that it was serious. He was as shocked as I was when I told him the diagnosis. From the following day - one year after I opened - I began to close down the Foundation.

I had more tests at Salisbury hospital. The doctors told me that they could not find any reason as to why the stroke had happened. They decided the cause was due to overwork and stress, and again they advised me adamantly to take it easy for a few months. The black oblong persisted, but they told me that over time my eye would heal until only a slight blurring appeared in my vision. During this period, my mind would repeatedly go back to the warning given to me by spirit. I was not to take my work elsewhere. I thought I was doing the right thing by keeping my personal and working life separate, but I only created more work for myself and less time at home. Once again, my guides knew best.

27

The Vicar of Woodgreen

Shortly after the episode with my eye, my doctor rushed me to hospital with a suspected heart attack. A variety of tests were done, but none of them showed anything significant, so they decided to keep me in overnight, just to make sure I was all right. The hospital admitted me to a special ward that contained mainly elderly people. Unfortunately, it was a mixed ward, and apart from me, there was only one other woman.

Opposite me was an elderly man wearing an oxygen mask. He kept removing the mask from his mouth and putting it on top of his head, where it would stay until a nurse came along to put it back again. Often, the nurses were none to gentle, as they would pull the mask out on its elastic and then let it go with a snap. They also shouted at him, as he seemed either hard of hearing, a bit senile or both. During the night, this man would keep calling me by name, which surprised me because I knew he didn't know who I was. When I told the nurse, she said that he called everyone in the ward "Ann", and it was sheer coincidence that it happened to be my own name. Elsewhere, there were other men getting out of bed and climbing into someone else's, or walking around without their pyjama bottoms on. It all seemed more than a bit sad. These men had probably lived perfectly normal lives, only to end up losing their dignity in their old age.

The doctors decided to give me another test the following morning and until I had had this, they did not allow me out of bed. Lying there, bored stiff, I noticed a number of beds with curtains pulled around them. Clearly, this was not unusual, but something drew my eyes back to one particular cubicle. As I watched, I saw the astral body of a man rising above the top of the curtain rail. He was still lying in a sleeping position and wearing his nightclothes. He rose slowly, stopped and then continued moving up a few more inches, before halting again. Meanwhile, nurses went in and out behind his curtains, and after some time, they placed his physical body on a trolley and wheeled it out of the ward. His curtains were left drawn and his astral body stayed where it was. I continued to watch, as he gradually rose higher until finally, he disappeared through the ceiling.

After some time, one of the nurses in charge of me came to take me to the theatre. As she pulled the curtains around me, I asked, "Has the elderly man in the opposite bed died?"

Looking at me warily, she stopped what she was doing. "What makes you ask that?"

"I saw his spirit rising above the curtains even after you had wheeled him away."

"Yes you are right. He died in the early hours this morning. We don't like to make it obvious when this happens, as it can be distressing for the others. We usually tell anyone who asks that they've been moved to another ward."

She helped me into a wheelchair and pushed me into the corridor. She did not ask me anything else, although someone had mentioned on my notes that I was a medium.

The doctors gave me the all clear, but they kept me for a further night before they allowed me to go home.

Both of these episodes made me realise that I needed to wind down. Reluctantly, I cancelled all my psychic work for the time being. Despite this, problems still reared their ugly heads, and one of them came in the form of our local vicar.

The vicar was new to Woodgreen, and said he felt it was his duty to introduce himself to everyone in his parish. Now, luckily for us, it was our turn! When he arrived on our doorstep, he interrupted a heated discussion between Pete and me, on whether we should move out of the village.

I invited him in and asked him if he would like a coffee. Sitting himself down, he said that he would, while he pointedly looked around my living room. I didn't mind him coming into my home, although I was taken aback when he said, "Some of the villagers have approached me to see if I would ask you to move from Woodgreen."

"Well, I am amazed. My husband and I were just discussing whether we should move out of the village."

His face lit up.

"And now you've made our minds up for us."

He smiled, and asked, "Have I?"

"Yes you have. We'll definitely be staying here."

"Oh no! That is not a good idea."

"I'll just fetch your coffee," I said sweetly, as I walked towards the kitchen, where I found Pete doubled up with silent laughter.

"Looks as if we're staying for the time being," he grinned, handing me the coffee.

"Are you coming in to talk to him?" I asked.

"No. I think I'll leave this one to you."

"Thanks for nothing," I muttered as I walked away.

When I handed the vicar his coffee, my cat wound herself around his ankles. Leaning down, he tried to push her away, but she would not have it. After a few moments, he crossed his feet and tucked them under his chair.

As I sat down I said, "Tell me about these villagers who would like us to move out?"

"There has been a petition with a list of people not wanted here, and your name is at the head of it."

"And why is my name on the list?" I asked, knowing the reason full well, of course.

"You're a witch and witches work for the Devil, so we don't want the likes of you living in our village."

"That is complete and utter rubbish. Who do you think you are, inviting yourself into my home and telling me to move? You've never met me before but on the hearsay of one or two small-minded people, you've judged me to be something that I'm not!"

"It's true enough. You are a witch."

"No. I am not. I am a medium, which is totally different. In fact I know very little about witchcraft, except I believe that white witches work with nature and help people."

He placed a small, black book on the table.

Tapping the book he said, "It's written here, in the Bible, that all witches are evil."

"I can't seem to make you understand. I am a medium, not a witch. The two are completely different."

"I've been told you practice witchcraft, and the Bible states that witches are in league with the Devil."

Enunciating slowly I said, "You are not listening to me. I am a medium. I help people. I listen to their problems. I give them healing. I try to prove that we still live on after we die."

Thumping his hand on the Bible, he said, "It also says here, that mediums are evil, and that they should not converse with spirits."

"Quite honestly, I'm not interested in your version of the Bible. It was written years after the death of Christ and is open to the interpretation of the reader. As Spiritualists, we believe that Jesus was a medium, because he gave clairvoyance and healing during his life and materialised after his death."

He appeared shocked by my answer.

I said, "You're supposed to be a Christian, and yet you have no tolerance of someone else's faith. Everyone has their own pathway to God, and yours isn't the only one."

"Your pathway leads to the Devil, not God," he stated. "Witchcraft is evil, with all the rituals you use."

I sighed. "So we're back to that again. I don't use ritual in my work, unlike the Orthodox Church which uses it all the time."

He looked surprised.

"Well, its true isn't it?"

He did not answer.

"How can you class someone as bad, when they devote their life to healing people?" I asked.

"You're not allowed to give healing to anyone. We in the Orthodox Church are the only ones chosen by God to do this."

My temper was rising. "I don't believe I'm hearing this. Spiritualism is a recognised religion in this country. We marry people in our churches, baptise the babies and hold funerals. You're so dogmatic in your own beliefs that you obviously don't want to listen to what I have to say." I stood up. "There's no point in carrying on with this conversation, I would like you to leave."

Totally ignoring me, he continued from where he had left off. "In our church we only have to lay our hands on someone to ask for Gods healing."

"Exactly the same as me then," I snapped.

He finally rose to his feet.

"Don't forget to cross yourself on the way out of my door," I said. "I wouldn't want you to be invaded by an entity."

Closing the door hard behind him, I leaned against it, trying to calm down, and then Pete came into the living room.

"Did you hear any of that?" I asked him.

"All of it," he said. "I'm not surprised the Orthodox Church is having problems attracting younger people. Can you imagine what it would be like trying to hold a serious discussion about spirituality with him?"

"Mmm, I've just tried," I said.

*

Later that week, we went to the village pub, and a friend of ours called us over to her table. "Have you heard the latest snippet going around about you two?"

"Oh, what are they saying now?" I asked.

"Apparently, you go into the woods at night, strip off your clothes and dance around naked," she said laughing.

"Then I feel sorry for anyone watching us, it can't be a pretty sight."

"What do you know about the vicar's hit-list?" asked Peter.

"It does exist, and you top the list. It was set up by two or three people who think they're better than anyone else."

"Are they local people?"

"No. They're people who have moved here from out of the area. They want to change everything in the village and they can't keep their noses out of other peoples business."

"Who else is on the list?"

"There's a young girl who has a baby. She is running a mobile hairdressing business. She has only recently started it, so she is not making any money yet. But they want her out, too."

"Poor kid. I suppose she's trying to work it around her baby."

"Yes, you're right. But the vicar, along with his buddies, is trying to stop her."

The vicar did not stay in our village for long. There were not many who liked him, and rumours circulated that he had reverted to being a missionary in a third world country.

28

The Pathway Changes

"For every soul, there's a guardian watching it."
The Koran

Along with my clairvoyance, meditation played a part in my life. I usually meditated by myself, but on some occasions I sat with other like-minded people. One day whilst sitting alone, a guide of mine called Abna came through to give me some thought-provoking views on Darwin's Theory of Evolution. The following is an extract from what he told me.

"The human being has no evolvement from plant or animal life, and both of these are also different from each other. There are many forms of life that exist, some far superior to us on the spirit plane, and who would equate us with the life form of an animal. None of us will ever be on the same level as these. We are completely separate from each other and always will be. Every single life form has originated from the life force itself that you call God, and it is to that life force we all return. Each of us lives in our own sphere of life, but we integrate with other beings, and those in turn, proceed to interweave with different forms. We must all learn to live together and try not to think of ourselves as superior, because we are not. You are limited to what you can conceive with the human consciousness, so I have to express this to you in a way you can understand. This is a little like an animal who can understand you with his senses, but who cannot read your thoughts."

I have often asked my guides about the world of spirit, but it has been difficult for them to explain what it is like. This is because, as Abna implied above, the human consciousness has to make the interpretation for us. It cannot always do this, because we need words to express a spiritual language. A language for which there are no words. Therefore, we are very limited in our knowledge of the spirit planes. When we die, we do not have a body, so our personality lives on a level where we communicate by thought. A spirit returning to me is "clothed" in an astral body. He does this by thinking of the way he looked and dressed when he was alive on a physical level. If he did not do this, he would be unrecognisable to those he's contacting. The same applies to anything else that spirit shows me. Providing it is something from our physical world, my consciousness should be able to recognise it. This should not be so difficult to accept when you consider that other planets in far-distant galaxies must have inhabitants. It would be foolish to believe that we are the only life form existing in the universe. However, those beings may not resemble us in any way - for the places and the circumstances under which they live will condition them. It is unlikely that our consciousness would understand them.

The spirit world is not "up there" or "down there". It intermingles with ours. It is a different dimension, which has other dimensions interweaving with it. Our scientists know that outer space consists of several dimensions, so we should be prepared to accept that our own world consists of different dimensions too.

*

In another meditation, my Native American Indian guide, Moth Hawk, contacted me. There is a special bond between us, for I feel as though I've always known him. I put this down to the fact that we work together so often that we have achieved a certain rapport.

"There is something I wish you to see, child," he told me in his gentle voice. He stood to one side and I found myself looking down on a scene of an Indian reservation. My clairvoyance changed to a close-up of a tepee, with an Indian woman squatting outside, cooking over an open fire. There were several children running around, playing and giggling. One of these was a small girl of about six years of age. As I watched, the flap of the tepee opened, and out stepped a young Indian male. He scooped the child up into his arms, turning her upside down and tickling her. The woman moved away from the fire to stand by his side, laughing as he played with the girl.

"The child is you," Moth Hawk told me, "and the man playing with her is her father - me - in a former incarnation."

The scene changed again. This time it was of a woman aged about seventeen, and she was dancing with a young Indian brave. I recognised Moth Hawk standing to one side, watching them. Many other adults and children stood in a large circle surrounding the couple. Then they too began to dance. When the dancing was over, Moth Hawk walked towards the young couple, and placed his hands upon their shoulders as they exchanged beaded necklaces and leather pouches. Then he took them into another tepee, close to the one I had seen before.

"You had reached the age of sixteen, child, and this was the marriage ceremony we arranged for you. You lived many happy years. It is not the only time we have been together as father and daughter."

Now I understood why I felt so much love for him. Whenever he draws close to me, my heart opens like a flower, creating such intense feelings that I have a powerful yearning to return to my spiritual home. This intensity of spiritual love in no way devalues the emotional warmth and love I feel for my physical family. Spirit has told me that some people, who live on the earth plane in families, or as close friends, often reincarnate together again. They don't always have the same kind of relationship that they had previously, or the same gender for that matter. The roles of parents and children may be reversed; and friends may have been relatives in a former life.

*

A small group of mediums and healers at our Spiritualist church asked Pete and me to join them for a meditation. After closing my eyes, my spirit guide took me to a large, white building. There were marble steps leading up to huge, wooden doors that stood open. On both sides of the doors stood marble columns, and the building appeared similar in style to a Greek temple. As I walked through the doorway, a man dressed in white robes moved towards me. My stomach turned over as I recognised him as someone I had worked with, many years before I knew Pete. The shock of seeing him in spirit, and dressed as a guide must have shown. He gave me a broad smile and took my hand, leading me towards a lectern standing on the left-hand side of the hall. On the opposite side stood another lectern on which was placed a large book in which a man was busily writing. He was dressed in similar robes, and he looked up at me, smiled and then returned to what he was doing.

Tom, my spirit friend, called my attention to another opened book in front of him. "This is a "Book of Death". Each person in the physical world who is due to die has his or her name entered here. When this happens, we know it brings sadness to those of you left behind, but to us it is rebirth. We celebrate with each spiritual birth, just as you do when a baby is born." He pointed a finger halfway down a page and beckoned me to look.

Only one name stood out. The name was Caulfield. Before I could react, he pointed behind him on the floor to several oblong, glass boxes that resembled coffins. "In these are a few people who have recently passed over. We let them rest for a while before we celebrate their return."

Each box held a body, male and female, old and young, as well as babies. They appeared to be sleeping peacefully.

"My colleague works with those souls who are about to be born into your world. He enters their names into the "Book of Life". Like you, we're unhappy to see them go, but you will celebrate their arrival."

He led me across to the opposite side, where I could see other glass boxes lined up. Expecting there to be a baby in each one, I was amazed to see adult figures of all ages lying asleep.

"I can see you're surprised there are no babies. This is because they are still in their present form of 'old souls'. Once the baby is physically in the womb, the soul will enter some weeks before it is born." He turned to me, placing his arm around my shoulder. "It's time for you to return Ann, as your friends are ready."

Tom walked with me through the doors and I could see another guide waiting for me at the bottom of the steps. Tom kissed my forehead and said, "I'll meet you in your dreams."

Slowly I opened my eyes, feeling as if I were emerging from a deep sleep. Then I remembered. My surname was in their book. I hadn't seen the initials, so I did not know which Caulfield was going to die. Each of us discussed our meditations, but I decided to omit the part that Tom had shown me. On our way home, I told Pete about our name written in the book.

"Well, there's no use worrying about it," he said, "If our time's up, there's nothing we can do about it."

We tried to put it to the back of our minds.

Some months later, Dolly and Charlie came to stay with us for a few days before Christmas. The weather had turned very cold, and although the central heating was on, we decided to light a log fire. As we settled down, Dolly stopped what she was saying and pointed to the grate.

"Look, there's a face in the ash of that log," she said.

We all got up from the table and went to look. There was no doubt about it. One log had almost burned to ash, and in the centre was a face. Not just any face. It was Pete's!

"My God, it's the spitting image of me!"

The face was moving as if in torment. Tears were running down the cheeks. I turned to Pete and his eyes met mine but he only shrugged. I knew that he, like me, had called to mind the things that I had seen in my meditation. We looked back at the fire and after a few moments, the face disappeared, leaving the ashen wood as it was before. All four of us discussed this phenomenon and we told Dolly and Charlie about the meditation. Despite trying to skirt around the name in the "Book of Death", we all knew that this connected to Pete in some way.

The following evening, we were watching television when the doorbell rung. Pete opened the door, but there was no one there. "That's weird," he said, "I suppose it was the wind, although that's never happened before."

A few minutes later, and we once more heard the "ding-dong" of the bell and again, there was nobody there. Settling down in the chair once more, Pete swore as the bell chimed for a third time. After checking the garden to make sure no one was messing around, he came in and removed the batteries from the bell-box on the wall. There were no more problems until the following afternoon, when we were sitting around chatting and the bell rang again.

"How the bloody hell has that happened?" Pete asked, rising and opening the door. "It can't work without batteries. There is no logical way that it can do that. But I'm going to strip the wiring from the bell-push in case it's some kind of fluke." Peter ripped out the wires and removed the box from the wall.

"I'll buy another bell next week, although I still can't believe it's been ringing without batteries," he repeated.

For the next few hours, we had peace and quiet - until our friends returned home the following day. We were pottering about, doing one thing and another, when suddenly - the doorbell chimed! We looked at each other.

"It's impossible. It just can't happen," I said. "I wonder if spirit is trying to warn us about something."

"It must be that: and I don't like the feel of it one little bit," Pete answered.

"I'll tune in to see if I can find anything out," I said, before walking into my psychic room. Despite my efforts, I came up with a blank. No one came to me, and I didn't get any awareness of spirit close by.

"Whatever it is, they're not going to tell us, so I guess we'll have to wait it out," Pete said when I told him.

Over the next few days, the chimes sounded intermittently, before finally becoming quiet. Once Christmas was behind us, these events began to recede in our minds while we got on with life. Then one morning in early spring, I stacked the dishwasher, turned the answering machine on and ran myself a bath. I was washing my hair when I heard the phone ring and the machine click on. Pausing, I listened to see who was leaving a message but I could not hear a voice. Oh well, I thought, it's obviously someone who doesn't like speaking to an answering machine. After my bath, I noticed the light flashing and realised that there was a message waiting after all. When I replayed the tape, all I could hear was the sound of the dishwasher swishing back and forth. Now that is peculiar, I thought. How can my answering machine pick up the sound of a dishwasher that is on my end of the line? After Pete came home, I replayed the tape to him but he was as baffled as I was.

From then on, it was one thing after another. The television kept changing channels, making it almost impossible to watch a program without interruption. Another time, I was speaking on the extension phone in the bedroom when a painting fell off the wall. On checking it, I found there was no reason as to why it should have happened, but I was aware that this was supposed to signify a death. The same thing had happened to my father shortly before he died. By now, we were both getting worried, and we hoped that the bizarre things that were happening around us were not an indication of a forthcoming death in the family.

We were both asleep when I felt as though someone had shaken me awake. I looked up and saw a round red light, the size of a large marble, suspended in the air above the bed. As I watched in puzzlement, Pete woke up.

"What's that," he mumbled as we both gazed at the light.

"I've no idea."

The light faded and we turned over and went back to sleep.

Spring gave way to summer and life was peaceful again, until late one night when there was a loud rapping on the front door. It was the police.

"We would like to speak to a Mr. Peter Caulfield," they said.

"That's me," answered Pete.

"I'm afraid we have some bad news for you, sir. It's been reported to us that your son has had a serious accident and he is in hospital."

"Oh God, no, what's happened to him?" Pete cried.

"It looks as if he was mugged. Someone hit him over the head with something heavy. A passer-by found him in the street and called an ambulance."

"Is he going to be okay?"

"His condition is critical, but there's every chance he'll pull through."

After taking down details about the hospital, Pete came in looking dazed and he told me what had happened. "It's too late to go tonight," he said, "It will have to be first thing in the morning."

When Pete saw his son the following day, his lad told him he could not remember much about the incident, and that he hadn't a clue as to his attacker's appearance. After a short stay in hospital, and against the wishes of the doctors and his parents, he discharged himself. Several days later, someone found him unconscious in the street again and paramedics took him to hospital, where, unexpectedly, he died.

Pete was distraught at losing his only son in such an awful way.

"Please, please, God, don't ever let that happen to me," I mutely begged. For losing a child must surely be the worst thing a parent could ever experience. God was not listening: for in my future, I would also learn the devastation of losing a child.

It was such a difficult and traumatic time for Pete and his family and I was unable to do very much, apart from giving him emotional support. In retrospect, of course, we could see why so many weird things had been happening around us. Spirit had been trying for some time to prepare us for the death of Pete's son. Months before, Tom had shown me our surname in the "Book of Death", but when I tried to find out more, I came up with a blank. If spirit had told us, what could we have done? There was no way that we could have prevented it from happening.

One morning while clearing up the kitchen, I became aware of spirit trying to make contact with me.

"Can you wait until later, after I've finished the housework," I asked with my mind.

The probing of the spirit fingers persisted, becoming stronger until I finally admitted defeat. Within seconds of closing my eyes, a young man came through to me. I didn't recognise him, so I asked him who he was and what he wanted.

"I'm Pete's son," he told me, "and I want you to give my dad a message."

I was surprised. I had only seen him once a few years earlier. This person bore no resemblance to the young man whom I had met. He had left home after I had met Pete, and he had gone his own way, only occasionally keeping in touch with his father.

"As I don't recognise you, you'll have to give me some proof of who you say you are," I told him.

"First of all, let me say that I'm sorry for not responding to your invitations to meet up. I didn't think there was any point at the time. Anyway, I'm here now, and I'm pleased I can speak to you like this, and if it's okay, I'll come back again to chat to my dad through you."

He then gave me further evidence about the attack, and a very personal message for his father, which I believed helped Pete through his grieving process.

*

This was a difficult enough time in our lives, without the added problems that the area gave us, so we decided to move house again. We had already made tentative plans to retire to Spain, so this seemed the right time to go. We put the house on the market and became busier than ever while sorting out the details that such a move entails.

During this period, I awoke one night from a short but disturbingly vivid dream. In my dream, a man was clumping down a hallway in a house. It was night time, and although there was a dim light in the passage, it was swinging erratically and casting shadows over the walls. I was standing in the centre of a small, dark room and feeling terrified while I waited for him to come through the door. In the corner of this room was another person watching me. The door stood open slightly and the moving light in the hall pierced the darkness. Ridged with fear, I was sure a monster was coming for me.

The footsteps stopped and the door began to swing slowly inward, and silhouetted against the light, was a man who was so tall that he had to bend his head to get through the doorway. Holding out his arms, he began to walk towards me. The light fell on his face - and it was Pete! Pain contorted his features and his lips parted in a silent scream. I turned my face away from him, towards the figure in the corner, who now came to stand between us. At this point, I woke up. Lying there in the dark, I thought about the dream. It was so clear that I knew it was psychic. However, it was so full of symbolism that I couldn't make any sense of it. I was sure the other figure was a guide and I felt certain we had trouble heading our way again - and once more, the trouble surrounded Pete.

Despite going over the dream with Pete the following day, neither of us could understand it. We wondered if something was trying to warn us against moving to Spain. We both thought that if spirit didn't want us to go, something else would present itself to stop us. However, we carried on with our move for the time being. We had found a buyer for the house, the removal van was booked and there were packing cases everywhere.

Pete had taken our dog, Rhea, for a walk across the forest. On his way home, he came across another dog wandering around on his own. He recognised the animal as belonging to the owners of a house that was some way back along from where he had just walked. Worried that the people were looking for their pet, he decided he would have to turn back. By the time he arrived home, I was preparing lunch. Now Pete was pretty tired.

As he told me the story of the dog, I noticed him rubbing his chest. "What's wrong love? Have you got a pain?"

"Mmm, I have. I had it twice whilst I was walking Rhea."

He rubbed his chest again and I could see he was sweating.

"What does it feel like?"

"It's burning. Probably indigestion."

"It can't be. You haven't eaten anything."

As I spoke, he clutched his chest and grabbed a nearby chair to stop himself falling.

"Oh God, what is it?" I asked, reaching out to him.

"The pain is worse," he panted. "It's spreading down my arm."

"Bloody hell Pete, you're having a heart attack," I yelled, running for the phone.

The doctor arrived within minutes, but by this time Pete was in agony. Grey-faced, he was semi-conscious.

An ambulance arrived shortly after the doctor, and between the doctor and the paramedics, they administered drugs to stabilise his condition before taking him to hospital. Pete was lucky. It had only been a small heart attack; and after a week, they allowed him to come home. Pete had always been fit, jogging on a regular basis and he had taken part in several marathons. Previous medical tests showed that his health was good and that he was an unlikely candidate for a heart attack. Looking back at this period, it is clear that for months on end, Pete had been under a lot of stress. I had been ill, his son had died and we were now in the process of moving. We fully believed that stress causes many physical problems, and so we both felt it was possibly our problems that had caused his heart attack.

At the time, we were too worried to continue with our plans for Spain. We had sold our house, so we had to find somewhere else to live – and quickly! Fortunately, we soon found just what we were looking for, and were able to move in almost immediately. Pete was incapable of doing anything physical, so I spent my time sorting things out and looking after him.

Our new home had four bed-rooms and it was considerably larger than our bungalow in Woodgreen. When Pete was on his feet again we set about decorating, which kept us both busy for some time. People began to get in touch with me for postal readings as opposed to seeing me personally. This was fine by me. I could work the readings around everything else and even work late at night if I felt like it. After a while, I found I had more time on my hands, but my readings began to drop, and then they stopped. Worried about this, I asked spirit the reason why.

Moth Hawk was adamant. "It is time for you to write your book, child. You have accumulated enough knowledge to enable you to write about your psychic life to date; and, more importantly, to address the subject of mediumship in a different way. You have acquired a vast amount of paperwork and we will give you time to put this in order in preparation for your writing; then you will be guided to a writing class. During this period, we will only send such readings to you that we know you can cope with."

After thinking about Moth Hawk's message, I opened my office cupboard and pulled out two large cardboard boxes filled with psychic paraphernalia and related subjects. This is going to take some sorting out, I thought. Most of it dated back years. I will make a start tomorrow, I told myself, and see where it takes me.

<< PART TWO >>

29
Using the Chakras

'Though you are poor in spirit or wisdom,
Do not say, "I am penniless,
So I cannot seek out knowledge."
Instead, bend your back to all discipline,
Purify your heart through all wisdom,
And in the abundance of your intellectual potential,
Investigate the mystery of existence."
Quotation from the Dead Sea Scrolls

In the second part of this book, I will discuss the chakras (the psychic centres) and their function, and show you how you can develop your psychic ability along some pathways by yourself.

Everyone is psychic to some degree and psychic power is a natural energy that is present from birth. It varies in each individual from a light intuition to the strong, dense energy that physical mediums use. Hundreds of years ago, we relied on this energy to survive, by sensing danger or when hunting for food. Advancement in the modern world means we no longer need to use our psychic faculties in this way. As man strives to better himself on a material level, he sometimes feels empty and unfulfilled. Now, more than ever, people are looking for answers to the meaning of life. Some people investigate different religions, while others – the young in particular – are turning to alternative means for insight and spiritual growth. People are now openly studying mediumship and the development of the psychic faculty on a personal and scientific level. Indeed, I have seen an article in a major newspaper to the effect that prior knowledge of events and intuition has now been scientifically proven.

Not everybody realises that Spiritualism is a recognised religion that has properly ordained ministers. They have exactly the same status as all other ministers of religion whose names are on the Home Office List. People can ask Spiritualists to visit prisons, hospitals or anywhere that someone is in need of spiritual comfort or guidance. Ministers conduct weddings, funerals and naming ceremonies (christenings) in the Spiritualist Church. Of course, you do not have to be a Spiritualist to be mediumistic, or vice versa. However, most mediums connect with the Spiritualist Church because there they can be among people who share their beliefs.

Even a brief study of other religions will quickly reveal that man is more than just a physical form. Since your spirit is a reality, the level of spiritual development will direct your physical life, even though you may not be consciously aware of this. As man is a trinity, his physical, psychic and spiritual bodies interpenetrate with each other. Therefore, the first positive step must be the acceptance of the psychic and spiritual bodies. The etheric or astral body lies the closest to the physical, so those who are clairvoyant can see it. Information transmitted from spirit to the physical, is 'clothed' in the astral body, to enable those present to understand what is being given.

Just as the major organs in your physical body are responsible for your overall well-being, the major psychic centres lie close to important glands and nerve endings. Your psychic and physical health are affected by the activity of these centres and their influence on the nerves and glands adjacent to them. The psychic centres appear as small vortices of energy, spinning around at great speed. The organs they lie close to convey impressions from the inner world of spirit to physical consciousness. Therefore, the amount of psychic energy received depends on the development of these centres.

Each centre, or chakra, has its own special function, and most people have one chakra that is more active than the others. In mediumship, one such centre may be the best way for spirit to use you, although it is important that you develop each centre to the best of your ability, to enable them all to work together.

You need to develop the skill to raise your vibration beyond the rate of physical matter, and to achieve an awareness of feeling, sight and sound that is not normally attainable. This raising of vibrations is a reality to those who possess a great degree of psychic energy. From time to time it will manifest, whether the psychic wants to use it or not, and often in the most unexpected way. Development cannot give you psychic power, but it will enhance your capacity to receive mediumship on a much higher level.

Although there have been some mediums who have developed their abilities on their own, it is advisable to sit with other students, and with a recognised medium in charge. In the early stages of training, you will make mistakes. You are exploring untapped areas of experience, and it is necessary to learn how to receive and interpret the information that you receive. The harder you try to still your conscious mind, the more thoughts and impressions arise from your sub-conscious. It is important at this early stage for the tutor to help you separate your thoughts from psychic impressions.

In the early stages of your training, you may begin to feel discouraged. Before you joined the class, your psychic ability may have shown itself strongly in interludes over the years. Now you will learn how to control the massive outbursts that you have experienced - and during development, these may now appear to be weaker. It is important to persevere, for your subconscious is trying to make order of the psychic influx, to enable you to tap into it at will. Once you have got past this stage, you will be in control rather than the other way round. So, always believe in yourself, and be positive.

The main chakras used for psychic development are only seven of the many smaller centres situated in the body. The seven chakras are divided into emotional and mental chakras. The emotional chakras are centres of "feeling". The first one is at the base of the spine. This area is where all your energy is stored, and you must learn how to bring this through each chakra, as they all depend on this base centre in some way. When you have correctly activated this energy with your mind, you will feel a physical sensation creeping, or even swirling, around in the lower part of your body.

The second centre is the largest of all. It is located in the area of the solar plexus. Through this chakra, you will feel all negative emotion. This is the region that mediums use the most, but especially in psychometry and physical phenomena. It is here that you will feel any kind of shock or disturbance, and it can actually produce various ill effects if you do not control it appropriately. This centre is extremely sensitive to emotional influences, but it does not give the definite comprehension of hearing and seeing. It is very dependent upon feelings, and only the properly developed medium can give a true interpretation of these.

The third emotional centre is in the area of the spleen. It works in a similar way to the solar plexus but the frequency is faster. It acts as a filter for the sensations, separating the good from the bad, and giving a more positive interpretation - although still through feeling. It is here that astral travel occurs, but if not developed properly, it can leave you with an awareness of being halfway out of your body. The closing down procedure used for all the centres is particularly important here, to make sure your astral form fits correctly into your physical body on its return.

Centre number four is in the region of the heart, and its energy is much finer than the preceding centres, although it still works on the same level of emotion. This is the doorway to the mental chakras, although it is still a centre of feeling. It is the area of compassion and understanding on a more positive level. The healer uses this chakra, so it is far more intense. The healer can pick up and actually feel physical sensations from his patient, and the pain and anxiety can be very real. The healer may be aware of a spirit being with him: even of the sex and age of the spirit, but this centre will not give true detail unless used in conjunction with the mental chakras that follow.

Psychic centre number five is in the region of the throat, and it is the first of the mental chakras. This is the seat of clairaudience, where one can hear the voice of spirit. Some mediums hear a voice objectively and describe the sound as coming from their throat. Others hear subjectively, on one side of the head or other, close to the region of the ear. This is similar to a thought, but it is much clearer. A thought will fill the whole of the head, but clairaudience will appear to enter the mind from the side without spreading further. It is possible for spirit to speak to several individuals at once, where they will all hear the same message. It is here that you receive clarity. You lose the sense of feeling, and you can pass on the messages that you hear. This chakra works with the spleen and heart centres in trance work. Developed properly, it is the clearest and most reliable area of information of them all. Investigators have discovered that this area can operate on a non-mediumistic level. They have discovered that painters, writers and creative artists of all kinds make full use of their throat centres, although they are probably unaware that they are doing so.

The best-known centre is number six, the clairvoyant or third eye. This is the seat of genuine clairvoyance. Much of what passes for clairvoyance - especially from the undeveloped - is only visual imagery that the person stirs up on an emotional level. Once you have experienced true clairvoyance you can never mistake it for anything else. The picture appears in a three-dimensional form. The medium can see all around it. He can see each mark, hair or blemish in detail. He can zoom in and make the picture larger or examine only one part. Once you get such a picture, the clarity of light surrounding the picture remains with you. Imagery on the other hand, is flat and similar to memory, without that special light and clearness. Clairvoyance can be either objective or subjective, or on occasions, it can be both. Subjective clairvoyance always enters the head on the opposite side to clairaudience. Once it does this, it immediately fills the whole of your mind, and you do not become detached from it as you do with thought. You are in the picture with the person or the scene that spirit is showing you.

The clairaudient and clairvoyant centres work together on a faster frequency, although one will be more dominant. Because of the speed, it can sometimes be too fast to hear or see clearly, but if you ask with your mind for spirit to repeat it, they will do this until you are sure of your information. Both of these centres support each other, and you can move from one to the other easily. Once developed properly, you will never mistake your experiences from either centre for imagination or wishful thinking.

Lastly, we have the crown chakra. Like centre number one, it is not psychic in itself, but it provides energy to stimulate psychic activity. The crown centre supplies the finer spiritual energy that is required for spiritual forces to enter. As the psychic force rises through the slower chakras, it awakens into activity a cosmic consciousness. It is as though one sees, hears and understands everything at once. Because mediumship is a calling, it is dependent upon the medium's willingness to work with spirit. It is at this chakra that the spirit of the medium, and the whole of the medium's psychic and spiritual development, blend and become one.

After psychic activity, it is important to close your chakras and cleanse your aura, to ensure that you do not retain any unpleasant conditions. This is particularly important for the healer. One must always leave the base and crown chakras open, as these are where your sources of energy are located. It is impossible to fully close off the chakras, but by making the mental application, you ground yourself back into the physical world again.

Always close down the psychic eye first. You will find your own method of closing down your chakras, but the following has been helpful to many mediums. visualise each petal of a flower closing into a tight bud. You may find that the petals want to close together. If this is so, then this procedure is too slow for you. Either let the flower fold rapidly or change to something else. Visualising a door slamming shut is very effective, or, with your mind, "push" the smoke-like energy back down through each centre. Whichever method is right for you, use it to close each centre, until all the energy is stored once again at the base of the spine and remember - this centre remains open.

When this is finished, visualise a white light above your head, and then mentally pull it through the whole of your body. It is possible to feel the energy of this cleansing light running through your fingers and toes. In many ways, the closing down procedure is more important than the opening up. This is because our centres open automatically whenever we do anything on an artistic level, such as reading, writing, painting, singing etc. They also open if you are discussing or reading about the psychic field. So if you get into the habit of closing and cleansing your chakras, you will feel more energetic and grounded in your everyday life.

You will have noticed that I have not gone into detail about the opening procedure for mediumship. This is because I strongly advise you to sit in a class or circle with others for your development. In this way, you will interact with your fellow students and have a professional medium in charge, who can guide you through most of the pitfalls. Sitting on your own does not give you the knowledge you need psychically or spiritually.

Each time you open your chakras your aura becomes brighter, and this light is like a beacon on the darker surface of the lower astral plane. If you sit alone, as I did in the beginning of my development, you may invoke psychic problems from which you then find it difficult to detach yourself. I must warn you too, not to become involved with Ouija boards, the tumbler and alphabet method of contacting spirit, or any other "game" that you use. Julie and I were lucky when we used the alphabet system, because our guides protected us from harm. Despite this, when Pete and I tried this method, we were told to "Go away", and when we did not do so, the glass smashed against the wall. Our guides were warning us against using this approach, because it is more likely to draw entities from the lower astral plane. Developing properly will not be dangerous. You will have a doorkeeper and guides in spirit who will vouch for those drawing close to you. Like attracts like, and you will only attract the type of spirits whom you would mix with on the physical plane.

When you sit in the class, you will find it hard to let go of your normal self or to face the embarrassment of appearing stupid. Remember that you are all learning, and you will not be alone in feeling like this. Nearly everyone is conscious of the way they look and act, and everybody fears looking ridiculous. Letting go of the ego is so important. It allows the energy to flow freely and for spirits to contact you easily. You are a bridge or a telephone line from the astral plane to the physical world, and it is spirit who relays the information rather than you. You are only passing it on, but as you develop, you become a sturdy bridge that they can cross over or the clearest telephone line they can find through which to work. If you do this, then your mediumship will go far.

30

Aspects of Emotional Mediumship

Auric Reading

A fully experienced medium can pick up your feelings through your aura when he meets you. Even if you try hard to hide emotions of sadness, he can still feel this beneath your outward exterior. If he then gives you a reading, he will always wait until those in spirit make contact before giving you genuine communication.

Nearly everyone has experienced some form of auric reading. How many times have you answered the phone to someone you have just been thinking of? Have you opened the door to find the person you are thinking about standing there? How often have you been able to tell if there is something wrong with a family member or friend, just by looking at their face or hearing their voice? Despite being aware of this, you probably didn't know what was wrong, only that you could feel it. This is because you have tapped into their aura with your own. You can connect with the aura of any person, no matter how far away they are. It does not matter if that person is in the room with you or over the other side of the world, because you can still make the link.

If you want to try reading the aura of a friend, ask him to relax and sit comfortably in front of you. You sit opposite, preferably in a straight-backed chair. If you sit in an armchair, you may become so relaxed that it will become too much effort for you to work. Tell your friend that you must spend a few minutes opening your chakras. Then close your eyes, take several deep breaths and relax each part of your body. Begin with your feet by squeezing them and letting go. Then work on the calves of your legs. Squeeze and let go. Work up through your body in this way, paying particular attention to your neck and shoulders, because stress collects in this area and makes your muscles stiff. Screw up your face and forehead. You will be surprised at how taut your features were before you did this. By the time you have finished, your friend will also be completely relaxed.

Now take your mind to the lower part of your body, at the base of the spine and between the hips. Try to visualise a smoke-like substance in this area. As you watch it, begin to stir it up with your mind, and see it getting thicker and swirling around faster. You may physically feel the energy moving over your skin like a gentle breeze. Now bring this energy up to the area of the solar plexus. With your mind "lift" it, and see it rising from the base. Be positive and "know" that you have done this properly. It is time to send out your energy to your friend.

Take your mind outward as if you are drawing a capital letter 'D', and pull your friend toward you, bringing him back into your aura and the solar plexus. You may feel a lurch in your stomach as you do this. Again, with your mind, bring the energy up from your solar plexus to the area of the spleen. See that smoke-like substance rising. Once again, take your mind out to your friend, drawing him back into your own aura and the area of the spleen. Now, make that smoke-like substance rise to where your heart is. Swing your mind back out again to your friend and bring him into your aura through your heart chakra. At this point you will feel as though you are expanding, and there will be other small sensations that you did not feel before you begun this exercise. Again, gently swing out with your mind to your friend, bringing his aura back and through from the base of the spine to the heart centre. Do this several times.

You are now ready to begin your auric reading. Whatever pictures you can see in your mind, describe them to your friend. Tell him how you are feeling. Give him time to answer. It is important to say everything you see and feel, no matter how daft it may sound to you. Until you "let go" of yourself, nothing else will be able to come in.

Auric reading cannot tell the future, only the past and present, so if your friend cannot understand what you have said, do not tell him that it will happen. Just let it go, and move on with something else. After a while, you will feel yourself straining to see something, and each time you speak, the energy will drop a little. So stir up the energy once more, draw in your friend's aura and bring it through your body to your heart centre again. After about half hour to an hour, you will feel depleted, so you should close down your chakras and cleanse your aura.

With your mind, see the smoke-like substance receding from the heart centre to the spleen. Imagine a door closing over the chest area. Push the energy down again to the solar plexus and close a door over the area of the spleen. Push the energy down to the base of the spine and close a door over the solar plexus. This is the largest psychic centre in the body, so it is harder to close. Double-check that your "door" firmly shuts. Leave the energy at the base of the spine and do not close it off. Now try to visualise yourself switching on a white light above your head. See it flooding your whole body, running through your arms and legs and into the floor. This will leave you feeling physically grounded again. Although this will seem complicated to begin with, it will not take long to get the hang of it, and you will soon be able to do the exercise much faster.

I would advise you to try these only two or three times a week at the most to begin with, because you will feel tired and depleted of energy if you do it more often. It is important to always relax properly beforehand, and make sure you open each chakra thoroughly before you start. By working with your psychic centres in this way, mistakes are unlikely to happen, as you will be in control of what you are doing. Thinking about your achievement will induce your psychic centres to open, so if this happens close down and bring the light through your aura.

Psychometry

Psychometry works in the same way as auric reading, but you achieve it through holding an article. Everything in the physical world has its own aura and an experienced psychometrist can easily read the emanations flowing from these. Since most people demonstrate psychometry on a personal level, the article that you hold will make the owner's personal problems evident.

The psychic will pick up the emanations of the person who owns the ring or other object, but if another person has previously worn the object, the psychic may well pick up feelings from that person instead - or a mixture of both. The thoughts and feelings of the previous owner may be stronger, thus over-shadowing those of the second. This is a little like dark paint showing through a lighter colour. If this happens, the sitter should make an effort to find out information regarding the former owner in order to confirm the reading.

Although this level of awareness cannot provide spiritual communication, once developed it can be extremely accurate, as I demonstrated with the stone from Biddy Early. Other developed psychics such as Peter Hurkos have had outstanding success, finding psychometry an invaluable tool in their work with the police. If you wish to try this method, you should once again begin with the help of a friend.

Ask your friend to bring you an article, the history of which he knows about. If the article is not his, he should not handle it too much or he will contaminate it by transferring his own feelings to it. Instead, he should place it in some white paper (kitchen roll will do), place it in a paper bag or envelope and leave it wrapped on the table until you are ready to touch it. Before you handle the article, give your friend a pen and paper to jot down what you say, and then wash your hands thoroughly under running water to remove any other emanations from your skin. Dry your hands with a clean towel or paper. As before, sit down and unwind. Try not to think about what you are doing. Note the way you are feeling. Are you hot, cold or nervous? Be aware of any feelings that you have.

Now relax thoroughly in the same way as for auric reading. Open up your chakras, starting with the base centre. See your energy again as a smoke-like substance. With your mind, bring it up from the base chakra to the solar plexus. Do not swing out to your friend, because you do not want his aura in yours. Go back to the base of your spine and bring the energy up through the solar plexus to the spleen area. Take your mind back down and bring this smoke-like substance up again through the solar plexus and the spleen to the heart centre. Once you have done this, repeat the exercise several times, gently running the energy straight through from the base centre to the heart.

Now you are ready. Remove the article from its wrapping and hold it gently in the palms of both hands. Once more, take your energy from the base of the spine up to the heart. Swing it out in a capital "D" to the article and bring the energy back into your own aura. This vibration is fast, so you must say immediately how you are feeling and what you are seeing from the moment you touch the article. Are you feeling different from the time when you took note of how you felt, before you started?

Has the article become hot? Does it vibrate? Can you see a colour, a person, a house? Every time you speak, the scene and feelings will change. State what you feel. Never add to it. If you feel nauseous, do not say "You've been sick," as you will undoubtedly be wrong. Each time you speak, you should swing out with your mind to the article and bring the energy back into your own aura. This will all seem quite slow at first, but with practice it will become faster and easier to do. You will know when you have had enough, as your energy will fade. When this happens, wash your wrists and hands again under running water. Use the closing down and cleansing procedure for your aura, because it is very easy to keep any negative feelings you may have transferred from the article to yourself.

If you are successful, you may have the makings of a very good psychometrist. However, it is vital to remember to pass on exactly what you see and feel and to never add anything of your own. If you are unsure of what you are experiencing, then say so. The emotional centres do not have the clarity of spiritual communication, therefore, always be honest. When you take a little notice of what you feel through touch in this way, you will be surprised at what you see.

Flower Clairsentience
This is another form of psychometry, but a flower's emanations are much faster than those given off by an inanimate object. A good psychometrist will be able to see and feel the birth of the flower itself. He will feel warmth from the sun, rain, earth and the activity and movement of insects. Even the negative sensation of being pulled or cut, can tug at the solar plexus. However, the majority of people who bring a flower usually want it read on a personal level, and this form of psychometry will reveal the higher aspects of the person who has held the flower.

The heart centre is more active here, working on the spiritual needs of the individual rather than the physical and material conditions. Holding a flower can help the medium trace important events in a person's life, which will show the spiritual growth they have attained. When asking people to bring a flower, I have found they often choose one suited to their own vibrations, even though they are not aware of this. In one class, I asked each student to bring a flower and to place it on a table without me seeing them. When I began to psychometrise the flowers, I found a small, purple violet gave off the highest spiritual qualities. It further revealed that one of the men had brought this in. His personality came across as a practical, no-nonsense type, but inside, he was clearly harbouring a compassionate spirit. He went on to develop into a first-class medium and teacher. Flower clairsentience can show the hidden mediumistic abilities of another person, or even a more conventional religious pathway.

To try this method of psychometry, ask a friend to bring a flower instead of an article. Advise him to hold it for a few moments before placing it on clean, white paper. You should then open your centres as described previously and draw the flower into your aura. This frequency is much faster, so the pictures and feelings you experience will change rapidly. Only the past and present will reveal itself. Only comment on what you see or feel. When you have finished, wash your hands and wrists, and then close and cleanse your chakras.

31

Astral Travel and Out-of-Body Experiences

Astral Travel

The third centre, which lies in the region of the spleen, is the main area where astral travel takes place. As a child, I accepted astral travel as a natural part of my existence. It was only when I discovered through my friends that other people did not do this, that I consciously made the effort to prevent it from happening. I didn't want to be different from others at that time, and I did not realise until later that many other people can and do travel this way at will.

The astral body is a replica of the physical, but it is made of a much finer substance that is invisible to the naked eye. When one releases the astral body from the physical body, it remains connected to the head of the body via a cord. This enables the astral body to stretch over long distances. The astral cord usually gives the appearance of being either silver or golden, although others have described it as a shimmering light. It only disconnects from the physical body at the moment of death.

When I was young, I often found myself out of my body, though I did not explore very far, only taking trips around the house or garden. In the physical world, my parents would tell me not to stray too far or to speak to strangers, so maybe this advice and instinct prevented me from venturing outside of those boundaries whilst in my astral form. Most of the time, I would be aware of when an

OBE was about to begin. At first, I would see a small flash of lilac light, which quickly expanded into a swirling mist that filled my bedroom. Then the beautiful lilac mist revolved, forming a tunnel with a small golden light that I could see in the distance. I would be drawn out of my body through the tunnel towards the light. At times, I would find myself experiencing the paralysing stage, which happens before the astral form is completely free of the physical. I have always found this to be unpleasant, and I have put this down to the fact that I am not in control of what is happening. This doesn't work in the same way with every traveller. Many people simply leave and return to their physical body without encountering this paralysis stage.

I still experience OBE's, and the lilac mist still fills my bedroom in the same way. However, if I do not want it to happen, I get out of bed and walk around until the mist disappears. At other times, I wake half way through an OBE and can be either in the paralysing stage or past it. I decided long ago that this was one area of psychic development I was not meant to be involved in, and I concentrated instead on my mediumship.

If you wish to try to develop this for yourself, it is very important to prepare thoroughly beforehand. The most significant aspect is that you are not disturbed in any way. Only try to experiment if you are certain that no one will knock on your door or ring the bell. Take your phone off the hook, and don't have any animals in the room with you. Once you are sure of peace and quiet, go to your bedroom, get onto the bed and lie on your back. Take several deep breaths and relax each part of your body, beginning with your feet. When fully relaxed, your mouth should drop open a little. If at this stage you have not fallen asleep, a few moments will pass until you find yourself entering a cataleptic state. As this happens, tell yourself you are rising in the air. You may feel reluctant at this point to take it further. This is natural, but it will prevent your astral form from leaving. It is important to overcome this instinct, because each time you try you will find it becomes easier to do. It is during the cataleptic stage that you may notice colours. Many mediums are aware of vivid colours before and during an OBE, so if this happens you will know you are succeeding with the exercise. At first, you may only rise a few inches, but with practice, it will not be long before you are looking down on yourself from the ceiling.

If you become aware that your astral form is still in a horizontal position, just "think" yourself upright. Once again, it may take a little while to achieve this. You will need to be several feet away from your body before you are able to move around at will, so this will take some practice. When you want to come back, you must make sure you align yourself properly with your physical body. If you do not do this, you will have the uncomfortable awareness of being only half in, and this will make you feel irritable and unsure of what is going on around you. After you have returned to your physical body, lie quietly for a few moments. Close your chakras, before bringing the white light through the top of your head. Do this several times. Not only does this cleanse your astral body, it will help to realign it as well.

Once you have succeeded in these experiments, you should take note of your surroundings. Look at your physical self on the bed and then look at your astral body. Check if you can see the cord or the light. When you feel able to take this further, you will find you can walk through walls, closed doors or go up through the ceiling.

There are many recorded incidents regarding operations. Some people have watched themselves during the procedure; they could see what was going on there, they remember hearing the operating staff's conversations and seeing the instruments that they were using. One friend, who had perfected the art of leaving his body, told me he would visit me at a certain time on one particular evening. Although I didn't see him, some invisible force knocked my lampshade violently and I felt some unseen figure rushing past me and out through the wall of my room.

Those who wish to take astral travel seriously can explore many avenues. I cannot stress strongly enough that you should take as many precautions as possible to ensure that you are not disturbed. If you are, you will suddenly whip back into the physical and you will feel very distressed. Astral travel can be a very exciting area of discovery, but like physical exploration, it holds dangers for the unprotected. Always ask your spirit friends, relatives or guides to watch over you whilst you are investigating the astral plane. You may even meet up with them on your journey. Never spend too long out of your body or stray far away. Remember, your physical body is lying in a cataleptic state on the bed, and if someone were to burst into your room, they may well think you have died!

If anything like this were to happen, you will still be able to return to the physical, but you may feel unwell afterwards because of the fright it has caused you. It is so important to take all the precautions, and if you do, you will find this a fascinating and rewarding experiment.

32
Training and Techniques

Meditation

Meditation is excellent for relaxation even if you do not wish to pursue any level of psychic awareness. However, if you do wish it, meditation will help you to achieve this more rapidly. I meditate on a regular basis. However, much of the time it does lead me into clairvoyance or even an out-of-body experience. Whatever happens and no matter what worries I have, I always feel relaxed and refreshed afterwards.

The important thing with meditation is to concentrate on one thing in your mind. You will never be able to stop your thoughts, and at first, you will find your mind straying from your object of concentration. Find somewhere comfortable and sit with your eyes closed. Relax your body using the method previously described. Then visualise an object that suits you best. This can be a flower, a cross, a light, a crystal, a candle flame – anything at all. Keep looking at this with your mind. You will find yourself thinking of other things but as soon as this happens, bring your inner vision back to the object again. All you have to do is repeat this until you are able to hold the picture of your object for a longer time. You will know when you have had enough. Open your eyes and slowly stretch each part of your body. You should feel as though you have woken from a deep sleep. Once you are up and moving around, you will feel refreshed and energetic. Check the time to see how long this exercise has taken. I think you will be surprised to find it took longer than you thought.

As you practice this on a regular basis, (each day if you wish), you will find your thoughts will stray less and less. If you are mediumistic, you may have a subtle awareness of spirit around you, even though you cannot see or hear anything specific. Acknowledge this presence and send the spirits your love. With patience and over a period of time this will become stronger, until you can see spirit in your mind or hear them inside your head. If this happens, you may wish to develop your abilities to become a medium.

If you find it difficult to concentrate, a physical object will help. A candle flame is always good to meditate on and many people prefer to use this method. Alternatively, place a flower or a crystal in your field of vision. Once you are relaxed, open your eyes and look at the object. Close your eyes and the image will appear in your mind. Open and look again, repeating the exercise several times. Make sure you do not strain. Always be relaxed. Gradually you will find that your eyes will stay shut as you concentrate longer on the image.

Meditation will help you to make clearer decisions in your personal and business life. You will feel less tired and you will have more energy and better health.

Zenner Cards

ESP or Extra Sensory Perception is a form of clairvoyance that one can test by using ESP cards designed in 1930 by Carl Zenner in America. Zenner used a set of twenty-five cards with a design of five different pictures repeated throughout the rest of the cards. These cards were one method of testing people in scientific studies to see how psychic they were. One person called the "sender" sat in front of another person called the "receiver". The tester held each card in his hand and asked the student to write down what design he thought was on the card. He used all twenty-five cards before calculating the score. When he wished to achieve a psychic score on any one person, he repeated the test several times. You can buy Zenner cards today, but there is no need to do so at this stage. This test usually works better if you have a group of people to try this out.

Get some white card and cut it into twenty-five squares. Using a black marker pen, draw a simple illustration on each of five cards; then repeat each illustration five times until all the cards are illustrated. The drawings can be of whatever you choose, but Zenner himself chose the following: a circle, cross, star, wiggly lines and a square. Do not make them too complicated. Choose someone to be the "sender" and someone else as the "receiver". It is not necessary to try to open your chakras, although it is to your advantage if you do. However, it is important for you to be relaxed. The sender should shuffle the cards, and then hold one in front of him. He should try to transmit the picture to the receiver. The receiver should then try to draw a picture of anything that immediately comes into his mind.

Use the whole pack before checking the receiver's illustrations and calculating the score. If the score is consistently high, then you should perhaps think about taking other tests connected with your psychic ability.

Editor's note: If this does not work particularly well, there is no need to consider yourself useless or as psychic as a brick. Emotion drives psychism, which is why it is easier to tune into an emotional situation than a cold, unemotional scientific experiment.

Healing

The fourth chakra lies in the region of the heart and one uses this for healing. A kind of positive energy derives from this emotional centre. It is the gateway to the faster mental chakras that follow, and works in conjunction with centre five in the region of the throat.

Many people are natural healers without being aware of this fact. Simply sending out thoughts of compassion for another person will activate this chakra, allowing the positive energy to flow from the healer to the sick person. When we ask in prayer for God to make a loved one better, we are sending out our healing energy. Often this appears to work, but at other times, it does not; we then become dejected, often denying the very God we turned to in the first place. There are many reasons for this. Perhaps that person should not be responsive to healing because they have chosen to come to earth to work through that particular Karma. It may be due to old age or because the body has gone too far to be healed. However, healing will always work on some level. If not physically, it may work emotionally, psychologically or spiritually.

Undeveloped healers find that people come to them naturally and tell them all their troubles. When on a bus or train that is almost empty, someone will come and sit beside them, unknowingly drawn to their healing power. Often when this happens, the healer will feel quite drained, because the other person will have depleted him of his natural healing energy. Development in a class will show you how to protect yourself from this.

At other times, you may notice that you have the ability to pick up the moods and temperaments of others, knowing instinctively when someone is telling the truth or not. If you wish to develop your healing further, it is important to sit in a class to enable you to achieve the most from your mediumship. This way, you will build up a rapport with your spirit helpers, and gain far more from the knowledge they will impart.

Some healers tend to dissociate themselves from trained mediumship, because they think that the energy they are using is different. Healing power is psychic energy, and the natural healer can draw this vitality into himself before releasing it into the auric field of anyone who is in need. When working with a sick person, the healer often feels the patient's pain and discomfort for himself. This can help on a psychological level, because in this way, the patient knows that the healer is in tune with him and that he can trust him implicitly. The healing energy comes from the emotional centres and one can develop these accordingly, but if you also develop the throat chakra, the added benefits are tremendous. As your guides draw close to you, they can direct you with their thoughts. Many times when healing, my guides have given me further information which is helpful to my patient and which allows me a clearer understanding of their situation.

People frequently come for healing as a last resort, after having tried other methods without positive results. I always suggest to the patient that they try healing once a week for six weeks, by which time something should begin to happen. It does depend on the problem, as it can be deep-rooted. Sometimes patients do not respond at all or do not give it long enough. Others expect miracles, despite the fact they may have already tried everything else. At other times, the positive changes begin immediately.

As soon as the healer touches the patient, energy is released into the patient. Once it is over, the patient will feel very relaxed and generally more positive in his outlook. The healing should continue to work throughout the following days, whereby the patient may notice small differences in his ailments. Sometimes a patient may feel worse to begin with, but he will usually pick up quickly afterwards.

My brother has multiple sclerosis and I offered to give him contact healing. As I touched his feet, I could feel powerful energy running out of my hands and up his legs. He could feel this too but he began to feel sick and shaky, so I stopped the healing. Because he felt so awful, he would not let me try again. I explained that the energy was stronger because of his serious condition, but that it probably would not be the same at the next session. He still refused and I have resorted to sending out absent healing instead. This is gentler and it can take longer to work. Sometimes conventional medicine will make you feel worse before you get better, and healing often works in a similar way.

Absent healing, (or distant healing) is another form of helping. There are many ways of doing this, but it is always important to ask for help from your healing guides first. I have a list of patients combined with their conditions, which I give out to my healing guides, along with a mental picture of the person concerned. If I am unaware of what the patient looks like, I concentrate on their name and problem. I always try to visualise my patients laughing and turning cartwheels, to show they are getting well. When I have finished, I close and cleanse my chakras, because it is still possible to pick up a patient's condition through this method. It is generally better to give absent healing last thing at night, because the patient is probably either in bed or more relaxed, and therefore, more receptive at this time.

If you think you have healing potential, you could try absent healing first before committing yourself further with either contact healing or a developing class. Write down the names of your patients, along with their problems and then find somewhere quiet to sit. Take several deep breaths and relax your body before opening your chakras. When you are ready, mentally ask your healing guides to draw close to you, and know in your heart they are there. Follow this with the method that I use. If you feel more comfortable using another method, then do so. Some healers visualise each person in a golden light. Others see their patients laughing and dancing around. When you have finished the list, thank your guides, close your chakras and cleanse your aura. Ask your patients to let you know each week how they are feeling, so you will know if the healing is working. If you get results within a few weeks, you could then take your healing ability further.

If you wish to try contact healing, I suggest you choose a friend to work on first. Before he comes, you should make sure that your body and your clothes are clean, and that you do not smell of strong perfume or cigarette smoke. This can be overpowering when in such close proximity to the patient. Wash your hands and wrists and then sit quietly, relaxing and opening up your chakras from the base of the spine to the heart centre. Once your friend arrives, ask him to sit sideways on a straight-backed chair that has no arms, so that it is easy for you to place your hands on his back. You should have a similar chair to sit on as you work.

While you are standing up, place your hands either side of the patient's head. As you hold this position, ask your guides to draw close and to give your patient healing. Then stand or sit for the rest of the healing. Move your hands to the top of the spinal column and leave them there for a few moments. Then move your hands slowly down his back, stopping for a moment or two each time, until you arrive at the base of the spine. Return your hands onto the patient's head and mentally thank your guides. Close your chakras and cleanse your aura.

While you give the healing, you may feel warmth or heat coming from either one hand or both. Your hands may tingle. If this happens, check with your patient to see if he felt anything. It is likely that he will have felt warmth from at least one hand. You will probably find that he feels very relaxed at the end of the healing, and you should advise him not to rush around for an hour or two.

Once you become more familiar with healing, you will be aware of subtle changes within your hands. One hand will be dominant, either becoming hotter or tingling more than the other. In the presence of another person, the developed healer will move his hands appropriately to different places on the body, such as the knee, hip, foot and so on, although one can conduct healing for the whole body purely through the spine as shown above. Before your patient leaves, ask him to write down anything that may be relevant during the week regarding his health problems, and to bring it with him to the following session. After he has left, wash your hands and wrists again. Try this healing for about four or five weeks to see if you have any positive results. If you do, then you may wish to develop your healing ability further.

If you intend to work as a professional healer in the UK, you must first register with a healing association. The largest and best known is The National Federation of Spiritual Healers. This organisation has several thousand members. It accepts anyone who acknowledges the existence of God as the source of healing power. The NFSH is a registered charity and a focal point where aspiring healers may turn to for advice and training. They hold educational and training courses for probationary healers. Their head office maintains a register of healers in all parts of the country and they deal with hundreds of requests for healing every week.

Spiritual healing is a recognised therapy within the National Health Service of Great Britain. The General Medical Council permits doctors to refer their patients for spiritual healing, and NFSH healers may attend hospital in-patients who request their services. If you are interested in pursuing spiritual healing, you should contact the NFSH for advice. You can find their address at the back of this book.

33

Aspects of Mental Mediumship

Clairaudience

The fifth chakra is the first of the mental centres. It is located in the area of the throat. This centre deals with factual communication rather than feeling. There are two main categories, these being objective and subjective. Objective hearing is rare because it takes far more effort on behalf of the medium and spirits who do the communicating. The energy used is denser, and it requires some form of physical mediumship for it to happen. Despite this, most mediums have at one time or another experienced some form of objective clairaudience. Whenever I have heard voices and sounds outside of myself that have no physical explanation, it has always happened when I have least expected it.

One evening I was sitting and reading a book, with only my two dogs for company. I heard Pete's car pull into our drive. The headlights swept through the windows of the room and both our dogs jumped up to greet him. As the engine switched off, I looked out of the window to wave, but the drive was empty. Surprised, I sat back down and picked up my book again. A moment later, I heard the car again and saw the headlights flooding the room in the same way as before. This time it was Peter!

Not only did I hear and see Pete's car before it actually arrived, but my dogs heard it too. I believe I was in a particularly receptive state at that moment, possibly because I was absorbed in my book. How many of us become engrossed in a book but are still conscious of sounds going on around us? These sounds do not normally disturb our reading despite the fact that we are physically aware of them. What I heard and saw was loud and clear, and not just impinging on my consciousness. Why I experienced this, moments before it actually happened, is still a mystery.

One still, hot summer's day, I was indoors with Karen. We were talking quietly, when we both became aware of children laughing and calling to each other in our garden. We both turned towards the opened patio doors, but all the sound suddenly shut off and reverted to the silence that only a hot afternoon brings. It seems that despite our conversation, we were both in a receptive state, perhaps brought on by the heat and quiet of the day. Looking back on the incident, we are sure that what we heard was spirit children playing with each other, but as soon as we became physically aware, the clairaudience ended.

These are only two examples of objective clairaudience; and they happened spontaneously on both occasions. I have only experimented once with objective clairaudience, and I used a tape-recorder while doing so. After opening my chakras, I asked spirit to speak to me via the cassette. I then sat quietly until the tape clicked off. After rewinding the tape, I heard the words, "my name is...", but the rest was indistinct. The voice was deep, slow and laborious and loud static accompanied it. Peter and I replayed the tape over and again until we were sure of what was being transmitted, but unfortunately, we could not make sense of the name. I did not have the patience or the inclination to pursue this experiment, but there are many people who have obtained success in this way and who have received spirit messages by means of more sophisticated equipment.

Subjective clairaudience is a voice heard in the head. It is similar to a thought, but one that is very distinct from your own thoughts. It enters the mind from one side, usually close to the ear, and it returns to this area each time after communication. Normal thought fills the whole of the head and is there all the time. You cannot stop your thinking process, although it is possible to slow it down. When someone speaks to you via the telephone, you can still think while listening to what they are saying, but their voice will be contained in one small space of your head and ear. Clairaudience works in a similar way. You are able to think, but at the same time, a small area opens up in your mind, and this is distinctly different in sound and feeling from your own thoughts. It is here that the voice of spirit makes contact through a special kind of link.

All the voices are different, and an experienced medium will recognise some of those speaking even without the added aid of clairvoyance. As with an ordinary phone line, there are times when the voices are difficult to hear, but the medium can ask the spirit to repeat the information until he knows that he has received it properly and that it is right. Once he is sure of what spirit is telling him, he should relay the message exactly as he heard it and without adding anything of his own. Many times I have received a message that made no sense to me - but which did to my sitter. If I had allowed my own feelings to enter into my readings, the information would have been wrong.

Clairvoyance
Just as clairaudience provides sound that is beyond human range, clairvoyance produces vision in the same way. The clairvoyant centre is the best known of all the psychic faculties, and it is situated in the forehead between the eyebrows. It works almost simultaneously with the throat centre, but the pictures enter the opposite side of the head from clairaudience. Unlike the voices, they spread throughout the whole of the mind.

As with clairaudience, clairvoyance can be objective or subjective. Objective seeing produces solid visions that are indistinguishable from physical sight. This is how I saw the Angel; it was also how Nicky and I saw my father. On hearing Pete's car turn into our drive, I saw the sweep of headlights in our room, which is what made the whole experience so real. On another occasion, I was walking my dog around the perimeter of a recreational field and following a man with a black Labrador dog. The man was small in stature, he appeared to be elderly and he was wearing a grey raincoat and hat, although it was not cold or wet. As I walked along, I became lost in my own thoughts, but was still aware that I was catching him up. My own dog, an Irish setter, had already run across the field. After a few moments, I realised that the man had disappeared. I looked around for him, but there was nobody else in the field apart from myself. I knew he could not have left the field because there was only one entrance and exit gate. He was walking too slowly to have gone far ahead of me, and I would have known if he had turned around to walk back the way he had come. I could only conclude that because of my contemplative mood, the man and dog were spirits.

With subjective clairvoyance, the medium can be surer of what he is seeing on a mental level. He can make these pictures larger or smaller, bring them closer to allow him to focus on one particular area, or enable him to bring his mind back for a wide-angle view of what spirit is showing him. The effect is three-dimensional. It is as though he is in the centre with the picture surrounding him. At other times, he feels suspended in the air and that he is looking down on a scene.

I often "see" spirit standing between or behind people. This is projected subjective clairvoyance. The figures are not solid, because I can see through them, but they do have a semi-solid quality about them. If I am with a group of people,

I often see spirit figures walking among them. Some of them will place their arms around the shoulders of the people they have come to see, although those people will not be aware of this. They do not always come to give me a message for their loved ones, but I am very aware that they are there.

One evening in my writing class, I became conscious of a spirit pushing between myself and another student. He was so strong that the sensation of him squeezing between us made me want to lean to one side to allow him room to get past me. I was trying to concentrate on the class but he wanted my attention so I knew I had to describe him to my friend. I quickly scribbled down his description and the message that he passed to me - both of which turned out to be accurate.

Unfortunately, clairvoyance needs clairaudience if it is to work properly. A medium can describe a spirit or a scene, but needs to hear why the person in spirit is showing him the picture. With clairaudience, it is not necessary to have a picture to confirm a message, although both usually support each other in giving confirmation. Out of the two vibrations, one is slightly faster than the other one. In my case, the clairaudience is faster. I usually hear a voice on the right hand side of my head just before I see a picture, although they often seem to come together.

On a subjective level, spirit can show itself to more than one person at a time. I once asked my students to visualise a pen. Afterwards they all gave me a description of the pens they mentally saw, and naturally, each picture varied in some way. I then told them to open their chakras, to ask spirit to show them a pen on a clairvoyant level and to write down what they saw. Each student described in detail, exactly the same pen.

To me, clairvoyance and clairaudience are the most important features, because they represent true mediumship. Communication is a delicate process in which all the centres work together to produce a mixture of pictures. At times, I feel a glow or warmth, or even a sudden happiness. It may only be a sensation of "just knowing" that spirit is close. Development will give you the ability to know when this is the case.

Emotional mediumship can be extremely effective, especially with psychometry, but we enhance healing through mental mediumship. This is the case, whether the needs are physical, psychological or emotional. To have the ability to see and speak to a person who has physically died, is spiritually the highest level a medium can achieve, and if you think you have this ability you owe it to yourself to develop it in the best way possible.

*

In addition to the levels of work that I have explained, there are other pathways for development. I have not touched on any of these because I do not have any personal experience of them. There are many books on the market on a whole variety of psychic subjects, and some of these are bound to appeal to you.

At the start of my life and its story, I knew nothing whatsoever about Spiritualism or any aspect of the psychic field, apart from what was happening to me. Through trial and error, I eventually found my pathway, despite encountering many negative experiences along the way. The two main things that I always advise against are sitting alone for development or playing around with the Ouija board. Both of these are similar, in as much as you are inviting spirit to contact you. By this means, any form of negativity will gravitate towards the bright light of your aura. I was wrongly advised to sit alone to develop my psychic centres and therefore, I attracted spirit entities from the lower level. I had a security system in place in my home and I would not allow anyone to enter my house unless I knew who he or she was;

yet, through ignorance, I encouraged undesirable spirits to invade my auric field.

As on our earth, all kinds of humanity exist on the psychic level. Thankfully, the majority of people are good, honest citizens, but there will always be some bad apples. When we die, our personality does not change. We are still the same person inside, and it is this part that lives on. Once in spirit, we have an opportunity to advance in the same way that we can here. The spirits who live on the lower astral plane receive the same opportunity, just as they would through our own judicial system. However, there will always be people who will not change their ways, even after they have died.

When I used the alphabet method of contacting spirit (similar to the Ouija board), I was lucky. My guides were watching over me, and up to a point, they gave me protection. There have been many instances of young people playing around with this method and having problems. These days, there is so much information concerning the psychic field, that no one should be ignorant about the dangers. As with anything worth doing, you need to cover the basics thoroughly before you go ahead. Once you do this to your satisfaction, you should then find out about a development class.

34
Preparation for Development

Before looking for a suitable class, it is important to consider carefully the reasons as to why you wish to develop your psychic ability further. Developing as a medium is a serious decision and you should not take it lightly. Once you have stepped upon the pathway, you are undertaking a calling that will be with you for the rest of your life. It will be necessary to surrender completely to the influences of the spirit world, and to become a bridge or a telephone line from them to those who are seeking help and support. You must learn to forget about yourself in order to achieve the highest standard of mediumship possible, and this self-effacement is perhaps one of the hardest things of all to do.

If you want to become involved because you think you can speak directly to relatives or friends who have passed over, then you should forget about development. If this is the case, then you should visit a reputable medium through whom spirit should make contact with you in that manner.

If you take the decision to become a medium, you should also first make sure you have the psychic energy necessary to go ahead. If you have seen an unexplained light, a flash of colour around someone, or mist rising from their body, and if you have heard a voice or had vivid prophetic dreams, then you are mediumistic. Any "hunches" or the odd happening that you cannot define in physical terms, indicate that you have positive psychic power. If nothing like this has happened to you, it would be best if you decided upon another direction. You can develop even a modicum of psychic energy to some degree.

Mediumship requires a positive attitude. You will be full of doubts in the beginning. Because your psychic power works independently of your brain, you have to assure your conscious mind continually that you are worthy. Spirit would not have chosen you if it did not think you could do this. Doubt and confusion are inhibiting to psychic development. Your psychic energy is a reality, but learning to interpret it on a conscious level requires training. When you are at this point, all kinds of excuses prevail to prevent you from taking the next step. So, dismiss your reservations and remain positive.

Do you really believe you cannot die? Do you believe that you have come into this life to fulfil some specific purpose? Do you accept this experience as a means for spiritual growth? At this point, you may wonder why you should consider these questions when you are only interested in developing your psychic energy. Any doubt about your own convictions will colour your development and cause you to question your achievements, thus delaying your progress.

You should speak to other mediums. Find out how they felt before their own development. Go to Spiritualist churches, as I did. Judge for yourself the quality of mediumship, and see whether you think it is good or bad. Tell yourself you can do better. How could you possibly convince others of the power of spirit, unless you are first convinced? Having said all that, there is no doubt that if spirit wants you to be a medium, trying to wriggle out of it will not work. If God and your spirit friends want you, then they will find a way - as I know only too well.

Your next step will be to learn your psychic mechanism thoroughly. Find out how your psychic power operates. This energy will activate on a finer and faster level of consciousness than our physical one. Communication registers via the psychic centres, which in turn transmit feeling and information to the brain. This shows the kind of mediumship that you are capable of, and which is the most suitable for you.

Healing power operates on the emotional centres, and it will not work if the medium tries only to develop the throat chakra or clairvoyant eye. It would be like using a hairdryer to boil a kettle - the heat is there, but the purpose is different. Thoroughly developing your foundation before you attempt to exercise your mediumship will save you tremendous disappointment later. You will discover the most accurate level for you to work on, and then you can concentrate in that direction.

I once knew of a mediumistic woman who had the ability to develop her healing, but she craved only to be clairvoyant. This longing prevented her from developing properly. She could have expanded her clairvoyance, which would have helped her tremendously with her healing, but she wanted to use it for giving messages. Spirit could see that her healing energy was the strongest, and that on any other level her mediumship would have been mediocre.

When spirit selects a person for mediumship, they direct the person towards a particular purpose. It is important to discover the right direction in the beginning, and then concentrate on being the best that you can be in the area that fits. Once you have considered everything and decided to go ahead, you should do so in the knowledge that you will play an important part in proving that we only die on a physical level. You can be that bridge from the spirit world to the physical.

Reading the Runes
Kim Farnell

We are pleased to advise that BAPS (The British Astrological and Psychic Society) and Zambezi Publishing came together to develop this project as the standard text for their Rune Reading course.
If you are interested in studying for a recognised qualification in Rune Reading, then you may wish to contact BAPS for further details. Their address details are given below.

~~~~~

Other courses available from BAPS, some of which are already accompanied by Zambezi Publishing text books:
Psychic perception ~ Astrology ~ Classical Astrology ~ Karmic Astrology ~ Tarot ~ Palmistry ~ Chinese Oracles & Feng Shui ~ Crystal Divination ~ Dream Interpretation ~ Graphology ~ Numerology ~ Practical Witchcraft & Magic ~ Introduction to Alternative Health.

~~~~~

Please address enquiries to:
Department **Z**
British Astrological and Psychic Society
P.O. Box 363
ROCHESTER ME1 3DH

~~~~~

Tel: +44 (0)906 479 9827
Fax: +44 (0)1634 323 006
web: www.baps.ws   **email:** info@baps.ws

How To Be Psychic

"A Practical Guide to Psychic Development"

Sasha Fenton

An authoritative guide, with information on everything relating to
psychic events and experiences, even including how to work in the
psychic field.

~~~~~

The book draws on Sasha's own long and successful career, as well as
those of many of her colleagues. Sasha covers everything from simple
techniques to the truly strange and mysterious, and she uses fully her gift
for explaining complex and esoteric subjects clearly and logically.

~~~~~

Every chapter offers hands-on exercises for readers to try for themselves.
Knowing how important, yet easily overlooked, they are, Sasha points
out danger signals and offers workable techniques for psychic self-
defense.

ISBN 1-903065-25-9   *£8.99*

160 pages

Prophecy for Profit

"The Essential Career & Business Guide for those who give Readings"

Sasha Fenton & Jan Budkowski

The right price for consultations...	Startup costs...
The equipment you need...	Building up your clientele...
Finances & cashflow...	Organisational methods...
Your spiritual pathway...	Psychic protection...
The Media...	Teaching & lecturing...
Stress and the self-employed...	A mental & physical health
The Marine Bandsman Syndrome...	guide...

~~~~~

Internationally recognised Astrologer, Tarot Reader, Palmist, Psychic and author with sales of over 6 million books; who else but Sasha could produce a guide like this one?

Together with her husband Jan Budkowski, who adds over thirty years of financial and banking expertise, their combination delivers the most authoritative - yet easily readable - work of this nature that any consultant could ask for.

~~~~~

If you're serious about your career, you need this book!

ISBN 0-9533478-1-8
240 pages

£10.95

Fortune Telling by Tarot Cards

"A Beginner's Guide to Understanding the Tarot"

Sasha Fenton

Sasha brings over a quarter of a century of experience with the Tarot into this comprehensive Teach-Yourself Tarot book, taking the subject all the way through from a beginner's standpoint to a professional level. Added to the usual Tarot book material, this new, revised edition of Sasha's 500,000 copy topselling guide contains valuable information and considerations arising from Tarot students' questions - in particular, how to overcome the problem of linking apparently conflicting cards to make a lucid, synthesised reading.

~~~~~~

Contents include:-

Interpreting the cards - why readings don't always work - spreads & their uses - how to link cards easily - what happened after the guinea-pig readings in the previous edition!

~~~~~~

Striking new Tarot card illustrations throughout, designed by the acknowledged historian and astrologer, Jonathan Dee!

ISBN 1-903065-18-6   *£9.99*
216 pages

Star*Date*Oracle

"Ancient Lore for Today's World"

Sasha Fenton & Jonathan Dee

Got a problem?
Need a quick decision?
Choose the right day for:
~ Getting a job
~ That hot date
~ Travel & holiday planning
~ Fixing things at home,
or planning anything else...

The Star*Date*Oracle highlights your best timing,
for any hour, any day, any year!

~~~~~

Also included:-
The LIST OF FATES reveals the destiny
in the name you use every day -
not necessarily your birthname or an unloved "official" name.

The MYSTIC PYRAMID unleashes your own intuition,
helped by your Guardian Angel, and gives instant answers to your
problems.
*The sources are ancient, but the system and results are
right up-to-date, easy to understand and to use!*

ISBN 1-903065-15-1   **£5.99**
192 pages

~~~~~

Our full, detailed catalogue is available at:
www.zampub.com

Zambezi Publishing
"Much more than just books..."

All our books are available from good bookshops throughout the UK; many are available in the USA, sometimes under different titles and ISBNs used by our USA co-publisher, Sterling Publishing Co, Inc.

<u>Please note:-</u>

Nowadays, no bookshop can hope to carry in stock more than a fraction of the books produced each year (over 130,000 new titles were released in the Uk last year!). However, most UK bookshops can order and supply our titles within a matter of days. Alternatively, you can find all our books on www.amazon.co.uk.

If you still have any difficulty in sourcing one of our titles, then contact us at:-

Zambezi Publishing

P.O. Box 221, Plymouth

Devon PL2 2EQ

UK

Fax: +44 (0)1752 350 453

web: www.zampub.com   email: info@zampub.com

(Want to join our mail list? It is NOT shared with anyone else, and is very sporadic - just email us your details, specifying snailmail or email preference).

Printed in the United Kingdom
by Lightning Source UK Ltd.
102384UKS00001BB/493-540